CULTURES OF THE WORLD

ITALY

Jane Kohen Winter

MARSHALL CAVENDISH
New York • London • Sydney

Editorial Director	Shirley Hew
Managing Editor	Shova Loh
Editors	Roseline Lum
	Goh Sui Noi
	June Khoo Ai Lin
	Leonard Lau
	Siow Peng Han
	Tan Kok Eng
	MaryLee Knowlton
Picture Editor	Yee May Kaung
Production	Edmund Lam
Art Manager	Tuck Loong
Design	Ang Siew Lian
	Lee Woon Hong
	Lo Yen Yen
	Ong Su Ping
Illustrators	Suzana Fong
	Kelvin Sim
Cover Picture	Terence Waeland (Life File)

Reference edition published 1992 by
Marshall Cavendish Corporation
2415 Jerusalem Avenue
P.O Box 587, North Bellmore
New York 11710

Printed in Singapore by
Times Offset Pte Ltd

Originated and designed by
Times Books International
an imprint of Times Editions Pte Ltd
Times Center, 1 New Industrial Road
Singapore 1953
Telex: 37908 EDTIME Fax: 2854871

Library of Congress Cataloging-in-Publication Data:
Winter, Jane Kohen, 1959–
        Italy / Jane Kohen Winter.
           p. cm.—(Cultures Of The World)
        Includes bibliographical references and index.
        Summary: Describes the geography, history, government,
        economy, and culture of Italy.
        ISBN 1-85435-453-1 : $21.95
        1. Italy—Juvenile literature. [1. Italy.] I. Title. II. Series.
DG417.W56 1992
·945—dc20   91–39165
                                   CIP
                                   AC

INTRODUCTION

FROM ANCIENT ROME to the Renaissance to the present, the culture of Italy has had a remarkable influence on the world.

A land of exquisite landscapes, dramatic mountain ranges and vibrant cities, Italy has attracted foreign poets, painters and novelists for centuries while inspiring its own artists—Michelangelo, Leonardo da Vinci, Botticelli—to create masterpieces known the world over. Today, Italy is associated with fine art, wonderful food, famous fashion designers and, above all, cities filled with buildings and monuments of historic significance.

Italy's culture is deep-seated. The family still plays an important role in the lives of most Italians and the Roman Catholic religion is still a significant force. The Italian personality is distinct among Europeans: Italians are known for their exuberance, their friendliness, their drama and love of life. This volume in the *Cultures of the World* series will explore a fascinating, creative people and their compelling history.

Rome

CONTENTS

Fishing on the Po. The Po Valley contains rich agricultural land, and farming here is intensive.

CONTENTS

The Palazzo Comunale in Bologna, a medieval building remodeled in the Renaissance, an example of architectural accomplishment in Italy. The bronze statue is of Pope Gregory XIII, a native of Bologna.

5

GEOGRAPHY

ITALY HAS BEEN PRAISED by poets and writers for centuries for its spectacular topography, dramatic cliff drops and stunning views. The landscape, however, makes it difficult for Italy's small farmers who must work with mountainous terrain and inadequate water supplies. The climate, although famous for its constant "sunniness," actually runs the gamut from freezingly cold to uncomfortably hot in many places.

FACTS AND FIGURES

Italy's geographical appearance is unmistakable on a map of continental Europe: it is that long, craggy-edged peninsula that looks remarkably like a high-heeled boot. France is to the northwest, Switzerland and Austria to the north, and Yugoslavia to the northeast and east. Outside the country's borders are the Mediterranean islands of Sicily and Sardinia, which belong to Italy; while inside Italy's borders are San Marino and the Vatican City, two independent states.

Italy has more than 5,000 miles of coastline. The country's eastern coast is on the Adriatic Sea while the western shore abuts the Tyrrhenian Sea. The Ionian Sea is to the south and the Ligurian Sea to the northwest. Sicily is separated from Italy by the Strait of Messina, which is less than two miles wide. Sardinia, on the other hand, lies about 120 miles southwest of Italy within the western basin of the Mediterranean Sea.

Italy has an area of about 116,500 square miles—a bit larger than the state of Arizona. It is approximately 708 miles long and ranges from 95 to 155 miles in width. Sicily has an area of about 10,000 square miles; Sardinia is slightly smaller with 9,300 square miles.

Opposite: **Santa Caterina del Sasso, a church and convent complex built in the 14th century, on a sheer cliffside on Lake Maggiore. Formed during the Ice Age, Lake Maggiore is the second largest lake in Italy.**

Below: **Italy and its neighbors.**

THE MYSTERY OF POMPEII

Italy is prone to natural disasters: damaging floods, severe droughts and devastating earthquakes. Both the Alps and the Apennines provide their share of large-scale earthquakes and small, but frightening, tremors every so often. In the last 10 years, thousands of people have been killed and many more homes damaged by earthquakes in and around Naples and the regions of Umbria, Abruzzi and Friuli.

Volcanic eruptions are still possible from Mt. Etna in Sicily and Mt. Vesuvius close to Naples, and from small islands off the coast. Probably the most notorious eruption in Italy, and one that has fascinated historians for centuries, was the eruption of Mt. Vesuvius on August 24 in the year A.D. 79 that destroyed the Roman cities of Pompeii and Herculaneum. As Roman author Pliny the Younger observed from afar:

"On August 24, at about 1 p.m., my mother pointed out to uncle an odd shaped cloud. We couldn't make out which mountain it came from but later found out that it was from Vesuvius. The cloud was rising in a shape rather like a pine tree because it shot up to a great height in the form of a tall trunk, then spread out at the top into branches."

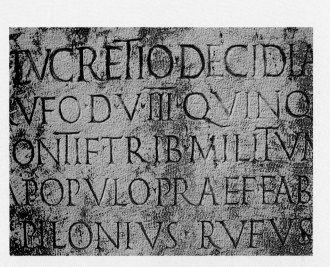

The volcano spewed ash and pumice onto Pompeii and, within three hours, had buried the city and many of its 20,000 inhabitants under *13 feet* of debris. (Herculaneum, on the other hand, was buried under lava and mud.) It was not until the late 19th century that meticulous archeologists began to uncover the ancient Roman cities. Unbelievable as it seems, they and many archeologists after them found that the carbon-rich ash had preserved Pompeii to a remarkable degree: entire bakeries were uncovered, ovens and loaves of bread intact. Elegantly painted frescoes were found on bedroom walls, thousands of scrolls made out of papyrus in libraries, statues and seedlings in gardens. Graffiti remained on the walls of public buildings offering such messages as: "The gladiators owned by Aulus Suettius Certus will fight at Pompeii on May 31. There will be an animal hunt and awnings will be provided;" or "Successus the cloth-weaver loves Iris, the innkeeper's slave girl."

Skeletons have also been found. Today, experts are able to reconstruct the bodies and lives of these ancient Romans by studying their bones. If the figures are intact, they can determine such characteristics as age, height, weight, whether or not the person was a laborer, if he or she was handsome or pretty, if a woman had given birth to a child, if someone was well-nourished or sickly.

The excavations at Pompeii and Herculaneum have greatly added to historians' knowledge of daily life in 1st century Rome, but much remains to be done. More than 50 acres of Pompeii are still buried and the cost of unearthing and preserving the cities' treasures is exorbitant. Unfortunately, the competition in Italy for historic preservation is great and the government money to finance preservation projects scarce.

MOUNTAINS, LAKES AND RIVERS

Three-quarters of Italy is either hilly or mountainous while the remaining quarter is made up of plains. Italy's northern borders are dominated by the Alps, which make a broad arc from the French border in the west to the Yugoslavian border in the east. The tallest peak in Europe, Monte Bianco (called Mont Blanc on the French side), is partially in Italy; it is nearly 16,000 feet high. The 15,000-foot Matterhorn, another Alpine peak, is shared by Italy and Switzerland. The eastern edge of the Italian Alps, near Yugoslavia, is called the Dolomite Mountains because the terrain consists primarily of a stone called "dolomite." The Dolomites are extremely popular with skiers during the winter months.

The Dolomites. The tallest peak here is Monte Marmolada, at 10,964 feet.

At the foot of the Alps lie Italy's largest lakes: Como (55 square miles), Maggiore (83 square miles) and Garda (143 square miles). From the western edge of the Alps springs the Po River, Italy's most important river system. The Po River Valley is Italy's most fertile farmland and flattest stretch of land.

The Apennine Mountains divide Italy in half lengthwise. They begin in the country's northwest corner and run all the way to the southern tip, in Calabria. The highest peak in the Apennines is Monte Corno, northeast of Rome. It is just under 10,000 feet. Mount Etna is part of an extension of the Apennines called the Madonie Mountains.

GEOGRAPHIC REGIONS, CLIMATE AND CITIES

Italy can be divided into the following geographic areas: the north, peninsular Italy (made up of the central and southern regions), and the islands of Sicily and Sardinia.

Venice, on the Adriatic coast, is one of the world's most beautiful spots, with its twisting canal "roadways" navigated by motorized boats for the Venetians and gondolas for the tourists, elegant Renaissance and baroque palaces, and countless squares and Catholic churches.

THE NORTH Italy's northern region is made up of the Alps, the northeast region of Liguria, and the northern part of the plains. The climate in the Alps can be extremely unpleasant during the long, harsh, snowy winters. Fortunately, the Alps shield the lake district lying just below its peaks from extremes of temperature. Both the Alps and the Apennines do the same for the Italian Riviera, on the Ligurian coast, which has a Mediterranean climate similar to that in Sicily. The area's most important industry is tourism. Its largest city is Genoa, an important port, the center of Italy's shipbuilding industry and the birthplace of Christopher Columbus.

The Po River Valley, or Po plain, stretches 280 miles from Turin to Udine. It contains Italy's most productive farmland, much of which is devoted to the growing of grains, especially rice, corn and wheat. The plain has a short but harsh winter and a lengthy warm season.

The plain is Italy's industrial as well as agricultural center. It is the home of what might be called the New York of Italy: chic, fast-paced Milan, capital of Lombardy, the country's financial and commercial capital and its second largest city. Turin, in the region of Piedmont, is another important northern city because of its connection to the Fiat auto industry.

PENINSULAR ITALY Peninsular Italy, dominated by the Apennines, is characterized by a rugged terrain and Mediterranean climate. The coastal lowlands are warm and pleasant, even in winter, while the highland regions in the interior get a good deal of snow. Much of the land in the central part is dotted with small farms, but the land is neither as fertile nor as well irrigated as that in the north. Principal crops include wheat, beans, olives and the grapes used to produce Italy's fine Chianti wines.

Central Italy contains Italy's capital, Rome, and Tuscany's capital, Florence—historically two of the most influential cities in the world. Rome is Italy's center of government and communications. Its streets and plazas, or piazzas, are filled with ancient buildings, magnificent sculptures and fountains, and graceful monuments. As the center of the Roman Catholic Church and the home of the pope, Vatican City, a tiny independent state located within Rome's city limits, is probably Italy's most visited site. Florence rivals Venice in architectural beauty. Its charming, twisting streets open up into elegant piazzas dominated by important churches filled with Renaissance treasures.

The seaside resort of Sorrento in southern Italy.

In the southern part of peninsular Italy, winters are milder and wetter than in the north and summers are warmer and drier. Much of the land is cruelly stark and dry and yields little to the poor peasants who farm it. Certain areas of Campania are blessed with good soil (enriched by volcanic ash) that produces excellent fruits and vegetables. The most vital city in southern Italy is Naples. Crammed with people, cars, factories and refineries, it is the third largest city in Italy and an important port.

SICILY AND SARDINIA Sicily and Sardinia share similar climates: very long, very dry, very hot summers and relatively warm winters. Most of the hilly terrain on the island of Sicily is given to wheat and bean cultivation and to grazing land for sheep. In the shadow of Mt. Etna (Greek for "I burn"), tropical fruit trees thrive. Sardinia, on the other hand, has few good roads and a harsh, mountainous terrain useful only for sheep herding and, occasionally, where irrigation is possible, for the growing of wheat, olive trees and grapevines. The capital of the island is Cagliari, a port city.

FLORA AND FAUNA

Because much of Italy's land has been cultivated for many centuries, little natural flora and fauna remain (except for what has been preserved in the national parks). In the Alpine regions, beeches, Norway spruce, and other conifers are present, while the lower altitudes are dominated by oak, chestnut, pine and poplar. Trees found in the northern lake district include the evergreen, cork oak, cypress and olive tree; in the south, the almond and varieties of citrus grow naturally.

Animals have not fared much better than wild plants in Italy. The Apennines are home to a small number of wild bears and wildcats (such as the lynx), and the Alps to deer, wild goats and a type of antelope. Some wolves still roam the hills of the south. The Mediterranean Sea, however, has a thriving fish population which includes sardines, anchovy, squid, tuna, swordfish, perch, mullet, shark and mackerel.

Palermo, the picturesque capital and port of Sicily.

HISTORY

THE ITALIAN REPUBLIC has been in existence only a little more than 120 years, but the Italian peninsula was called "Italy" a thousand years before Christ was born. The country and its many competing regions changed hands countless times in the intervening centuries: parts of it have belonged to the Etruscans, the Greeks, the Carthaginians (present-day Tunisians), the French, the Germans, the Austrians, the Spanish and the Catholic Church.

Italy has been ruled by great emperors, popes, monarchs, powerful families, Napoleon, the Fascist leader Benito Mussolini and now democratically elected presidents and prime ministers. The country has had periods of astonishing development—during the peaceful days of the Roman Empire, the Renaissance and the post-World War II economic boom—and devastating plague, war, poverty and terrorism. Today, Italy is among Europe's healthiest nations, in the economic sense, and its people maintain a high standard of living.

ANCIENT HISTORY

BEGINNINGS The first inhabitants of the Italian peninsula migrated south from Asia and Europe more than 30,000 years ago. About 4,000 years ago, the land was dominated by Latin and Italic tribes.

In about 1200 B.C., the first Etruscans appeared. Although their origins are difficult to determine, many historians believe they came from Lydia, an ancient kingdom in present-day Turkey. The Etruscans had a highly developed culture, with expertise in the areas of road building, engineering, mining, painting, sculpting, farming, sailing and warfare. By about 800 B.C., the Greeks and Phoenicians ruled the colonies in the south and the island of Sicily, and the Etruscans dominated central Italy.

"How much more Etruscan than Roman the Italian of today is: sensitive, diffident, craving really for symbols and mysteries, able to be delighted with true delight over small things, violent in spasms, and altogether without sternness or natural will-to-power."
—*D.H. Lawrence*

Opposite: **The Colosseum in Rome, built in the 1st century A.D. at the height of the Roman Empire. Here, up to 50,000 spectators watched gladiators fight wild beasts or other gladiators.**

The Roman Forum was the center of Rome. It consisted of a complex of government buildings, temples and shops, and open spaces.

The Etruscan culture had a powerful impact on Roman society. Etruscans had their own language (now lost); they considered women to be nearly equal members of society, allowing them to learn to read, to retain their names and to own property; and they were known and respected for their ability to predict the future. The man who foreshadowed the murder of Julius Caesar with the words "Beware the ides of March!" was an Etruscan. The wool capes of the Etruscans inspired the Roman toga.

ROME AND JULIUS CAESAR The Latins, with their capital in Rome, defeated the Etruscans in 509 B.C. and established the first Roman republic, which was governed by elected officials rather than monarchs. Roman society had a three-tier class system. At the top were the patricians, members of the aristocracy and the landowners. Next came the plebeians, the common people, followed by the slaves, who were not considered citizens of the republic. Patricians and plebeians were given the right to fight in the army and to participate in politics, but slaves were not.

The Roman constitution recognized the importance of allowing the people to participate in government. It gave the leader less power by making him answer to the legislature, the Roman Senate. In 454 B.C., the plebeians forced the lawmakers to develop a written legal code called the Twelve Tablets of Law. These laws, engraved on bronze tablets that were kept in the Roman Forum, had great significance for future democracies. The laws dealt with the writing of contracts, the rights of property owners, debt, marriage, divorce and the punishment of criminals.

By the year 272 B.C., the Romans had defeated the Greeks in the south and now ruled the whole Italian peninsula. In the century that followed, Rome fought in three Punic Wars against Carthage (now Tunisia). In 146 B.C., Roman soldiers set Carthage on fire and covered the soil with salt, so the land could not be used for agriculture. In winning the Punic Wars, the Romans seized Sicily, Sardinia, the island of Corsica, and later, Spain and Greece. By 63 B.C., almost the entire Mediterranean belonged to Rome.

In 49 B.C., Julius Caesar further expanded the empire by conquering Gaul (France). Caesar was a military genius, a talented orator, an accomplished poet and a historian. He was a member of the aristocracy but supported the plebeian cause. In 45 B.C., he became dictator of the republic and ruler of its vast holdings. Caesar believed in equality (he allowed all of Italy's inhabitants to become Roman citizens), but he also believed that, as dictator, he should have absolute supremacy over the land and be able to choose the next ruler. For this he was stabbed to death by a group of senators, including a man named Marcus Brutus, whom some believe to be Caesar's illegitimate son.

A statue of Julius Caesar in France, a reminder of the Roman conquest of the country in 49 B.C.

17

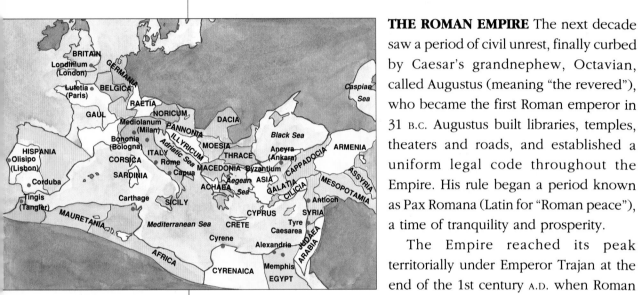

The Roman Empire in A.D. 117.

THE ROMAN EMPIRE The next decade saw a period of civil unrest, finally curbed by Caesar's grandnephew, Octavian, called Augustus (meaning "the revered"), who became the first Roman emperor in 31 B.C. Augustus built libraries, temples, theaters and roads, and established a uniform legal code throughout the Empire. His rule began a period known as Pax Romana (Latin for "Roman peace"), a time of tranquility and prosperity.

The Empire reached its peak territorially under Emperor Trajan at the end of the 1st century A.D. when Roman thought, customs, language (Latin) and administration dominated the land from the Caspian Sea to the Atlantic Ocean, encompassing everything from Great Britain to Egypt.

By the 3rd century, the Empire had begun to deteriorate. Christianity was becoming more widespread, encouraging peace rather than combat—what was needed to defend the Empire's vast boundaries. Moreover, the land was repeatedly invaded by Asian and Germanic "barbarians" (Latin for "foreigners"). In 285, the Empire was divided into two parts—East and West. Later, Christianity was made the Empire's official religion and the capital relocated from Rome to Constantinople (present-day Istanbul).

In the 4th and 5th centuries, the Western Roman Empire crumbled and fell to the barbarians—the Visigoths (from western Russia) and the Vandals (from Hungary). By the early part of the 8th century, the popes, who had great influence over the Italian peninsula, had caused an irreparable rift between Rome and the Eastern Empire.

DAILY LIFE IN THE ROMAN EMPIRE

Life in the Empire was highly civilized for the most part, especially in the larger cities, and filled with pleasures, especially for the wealthy. The homes of the rich were often large, 20-room dwellings with open central skylights, elaborate gardens, walls decorated with beautiful frescoes, living rooms, dining rooms and multiple bedrooms (for family members and household slaves). The ancient Romans ate three meals a day while reclining on couches in the dining room. Poorer people lived in small, one-room apartments and often got their food from take-out restaurants. Many Romans went to the public baths every day—to bathe, to relax with their friends and to play dice. Slaves in the bath houses served food and beverages to the bathers, gave massages and cleaned the baths.

The ancient Romans loved being entertained and they were avid theater-goers. Greek tragedies and comedies, high-energy farces, ballet and mime were popular, and audiences were allowed to shout their comments aloud as the actors and dancers performed. The Romans also enjoyed gladiator fights, where slaves fought each other to the death, chariot races and animal fights between bears, giraffes, zebras, elephants and lions. Sometimes, arenas were flooded so crocodiles and hippos could battle for the crowds.

Within a typical Roman family, the father was the absolute head of the household and his wife and children were highly obedient. The father was the legal owner of the house, including its inhabitants. Women shopped for food, managed the slaves and took care of the children. (The illustration above shows a Roman matron selecting a goose in a meat market. Women did work in, and sometimes owned, small shops.) Boys were favored over girls. All children went to small schools outside the home and were often taught by intelligent Greek slaves. In their spare time, children played with toys, their pets (cats and dogs were most common), small doll-like figures, hoops and balls. Boys liked wrestling and fencing. Family members often went to the temple to make offerings to the gods. Marriages were arranged by families when the children were very young. The marriage date itself was set only after consulting the calendar for an auspicious or lucky day, usually at the end of June.

THE MIDDLE AGES During the next 1,000 years, parts of Italy were successively attacked and seized by different invaders including Byzantines, Germans, Arabs, Normans, French, Spaniards and Austrians. In the year 800, the establishment of the Holy Roman Empire brought central Italy under the official control of the Church and cut off the north from the southern region. By the 11th century, the north was controlled primarily by Lombards, the middle by the papacy, and the south by Normans.

By the end of the 12th century, much of Italy was divided into many tiny city-states that had achieved some independence from their official rulers. The city-states had strong commercial ties with the rest of Europe. They were prosperous places, rich in culture and populated by successful merchants and highly skilled artisans. Many were run by rich and powerful families: the Viscontis in Milan, the Della Scalas in Verona, the Malatestas in Rimini and the Gonzagas in Mantua. Venice, Genoa and Siena were also strong, as was Florence, governed in the 14th century by a family of bankers called the Medicis.

A Byzantine mosaic in Istanbul showing Byzantine emperors Justinian and Constantine paying tribute to Mary and Jesus. The Byzantine influence in Italy was not only political, but cultural and artistic as well. Byzantine architecture and mosaics adorned Rome and magnificent basilicas were built in Ravenna.

THE RENAISSANCE Wealthy members of the merchant class were partly responsible for sparking the great cultural movement in Italy called the Renaissance ("rebirth") which had a phenomenal impact on Western European thought. Greek scholars were invited to an academy in Florence. As lovers of the arts, Italy's leading Renaissance families paid painters to paint, sculptors to sculpt, architects to build and poets to write.

Renaissance thought is characterized by its emphasis on the human being as the master of his or her destiny, rather than as a victim of fate.

The ideal Renaissance person possessed a great deal of knowledge about many subjects, both scientific and creative. (Leonardo da Vinci, for instance, was a highly accomplished scientist, engineer and artist.) The Renaissance thinker embraced the classical Greek idea of beauty and artistic perspective and lived by the notion that the human being as an individual could direct his or her life (business, government) in a rational manner.

MODERN HISTORY

FOREIGN INFLUENCES The Italian city-states lost much of their autonomy in the centuries that followed as the French and the Spanish battled for Italian soil. After the second half of the 16th century, the Spanish dominated most of Italy; only Venice and the duchy of Savoy-Piedmont retained some independence. Austria became a major power in the north after the War of the Spanish Succession ended in 1713, while the Spanish Bourbons dominated the south and the popes retained their hold over the central states.

At the end of the 18th century, French republicans led by Napoleon Bonaparte invaded northern and central Italy. By 1799, Napoleon controlled much of Italy and acted as its king. During his "reign," Napoleon made many improvements: he retrained the Italian army, built bridges and schools, terminated the feudal system of land management, took property away from the papacy, revised the legal system and restored many of Italy's roads. By instituting these reforms and by inspiring a feeling of nationalism among the Italian people, Napoleon gave Italy a sturdy foundation for independence.

The Altar of the Chapel of Princes in Florence, resting place of the Medici princes. The Medicis were one of Italy's leading Renaissance families. In 1439, Cosimo de' Medici invited a group of classical Greek scholars to an academy he sponsored for the study of Greek philosophy, thereby making Florence a center for the study of the humanities.

INDEPENDENCE After the defeat of Napoleon at Waterloo in 1815, the Congress of Vienna put Italy back into the hands of its former monarchs—the Austrians, the pope and the Bourbons—and the region of Piedmont retained its independence. In 1831, Giuseppe Mazzini, a masterful political thinker from Genoa, began an unsuccessful movement for Italian unification, or what was known as the Risorgimento ("resurgence"). In the mid-19th century, Italians turned to the leader of Piedmont and Sardinia, Victor Emmanuel II, and his prime minister, Camillo di Cavour, for a plan to rid their country of the Austrians. Cavour sought the help of France's Napoleon III and, in 1859, the Austrian army was defeated by French and Italian forces, and Milan and Lombardy were conquered. In 1860, much of northern and central Italy voted to unite with Piedmont, Milan and Lombardy.

Camillo di Cavour.

Giuseppe Garibaldi, a freedom fighter and ally of Mazzini, united southern Italy and Sicily with the north on September 7, 1860. Later that month, the papal states were taken. The only territories that remained independent were the province of Venetia (where Venice is located) and the city of Rome.

POST-UNIFICATION YEARS Italy after unification was unstable. Although the different regions were now administered by a central government, they were still distinct in language and custom. The nation had 33 different cabinets in its first 35 years, and many people were illiterate and even more were impoverished. Seeking a better life, millions of Italians emigrated to other countries in the next five decades. When World War I broke out, Italy at first remained neutral, but later joined forces with France and Great Britain and eventually lost 600,000 men.

MUSSOLINI AND THE FASCIST ERA After the war, Italians, frustrated, disillusioned and hungry, looked for someone who they thought could raise the national morale, revitalize the economy, stabilize the political situation and keep Communism at bay. They turned to Benito Mussolini, the son of a Socialist blacksmith and a schoolteacher, a powerful, persuasive orator and an ambitious, charismatic politician.

In 1921, Mussolini founded the Fascist Party and won 35 seats in parliament. Promising to keep taxes and inflation low, to control labor groups and prevent strikes, and to maintain law and order, Mussolini became popular with members of the upper, middle and lower classes. In 1929, at the age of 39, Mussolini was appointed prime minister by King Victor Emmanuel III in Rome. In 1925, "Il Duce" ("eel Doo-chay") or "The Leader," as Mussolini named himself, became the dictator of Italy. He outlawed all political parties other than his Fascist Party, censored the press, had his enemies murdered, dissolved trade unions and created an Italian secret police to deal with non-supporters. Democracy was denounced.

The Victor Emmanuel monument in Rome. Victor Emmanuel II was proclaimed King of Italy and its 22 million citizens in February 1861.

In an attempt to relive the great period of the Roman Empire, Mussolini expanded Italy's territory by conquering Ethiopia and its primitive army with machine guns and poison gas in 1936—much to the dismay of the League of Nations. He soon allied himself with Adolf Hitler, whose absolute power Mussolini envied. In 1940, he declared war on Great Britain and France. Mussolini's forces lost nearly every World War II battle they entered—in France, in Africa, in Greece, in Albania. The Germans, furious at Mussolini's repeated military failures, occupied Italy.

When the Allies entered Sicily in 1943, Italians greeted them as liberating heroes. Mussolini was ousted from power and was subsequently arrested, only to be rescued by German paratroopers and sent to an area of northern Italy still held by the Germans. In 1944, Italy realigned itself against the Germans. Early the next year, after the Germans had lost their hold on Europe, a group of partisans murdered Mussolini and his mistress and hung their bodies upside down for all to see. A few days later, Adolf Hitler committed suicide.

THE ITALIAN REPUBLIC In 1946, Italians voted to make Italy a republic and the nation's last king, Umberto II, abdicated after a 34-day reign. With women voting for the first time, the Italian people voted to give 35% of the seats in their new Constituent Assembly to the members of the Christian Democrats, 20% of the seats to the Socialists, 19% to the

Mussolini was obsessed with his public image. Always trying to appear strong and masculine, he stood on a stool to make himself appear taller at official gatherings and left his study light on all night—while he slept—to fool the public into thinking he alone was keeping watch over national affairs.

Communists and the remaining seats to smaller groups. In 1947, Italy gave up control of Ethiopia and in 1948, a new constitution took effect, officially reinstating all the freedoms that the Fascists had condemned and instituting a parliamentary system of government. In the 1950s, the Italian economy was resuscitated, thanks in part to financial assistance from the U.S. government under the Marshall Plan. In 1957, Italy became a charter member of the European Economic Community.

The 1960s and 70s, dominated politically by the Christian Democrats, were periods of continued economic

The World War II memorial. Mussolini led his country into World War II on the side of the Germans.

growth for Italy. The 1970s and the early 80s, however, were characterized by tragic acts of terrorism, primarily by a group called the Red Brigades. Between 1974 and 1982, hundreds of people—politicians, journalists, policemen and innocent bystanders—were murdered by terrorists who thought they could bring about social change through violence. The low point of the terrorist era was the kidnaping and subsequent murder of the former Christian Democrat prime minister Aldo Moro in 1978. Many of those responsible for this and other terrorist crimes have since been tried and sentenced to life imprisonment.

From 1983 to 1986, Bettino Craxi, the first Socialist prime minister, held reigns of government for the longest uninterrupted term since the end of World War II. Today, the Christian Democrats are again in power—Giulio Andreotti is prime minister and Francesco Cossiga is president.

GOVERNMENT

IN JUNE 1946, Italians voted to abolish the constitutional monarchy which had led the country since 1861, and to institute democratic rule. Today, Italy is considered a parliamentary republic. The country is governed by the constitution of 1948, which guarantees freedom of speech, thought and the press.

DIVISIONS OF GOVERNMENT

The legislative branch of the government, or the Parliament, is divided into the Senate and the Chamber of Deputies, both of which have equal power. The Senate is made up of 322 members (315 of them elected while the remaining members are former presidents and others who are appointed for life) and the Chamber of Deputies has 630 members. Some laws are passed by majority vote in both houses, but most are passed by small committees formed within each house. Members of Parliament are elected for a term of five years.

The president of Italy is the ceremonial head of state. Elected by the members of Parliament for a seven-year term, he has the power to veto a law, but his veto can be overridden by a majority of both houses. The president's foremost duty is to nominate a prime minister, who heads the Council of Ministers, or cabinet.

The judicial arm of government is divided into two parts: the civil and criminal courts and the administrative courts. A third court, established after World War II, deals only with the constitution. Italy's judicial system is based on ancient Roman law. Italian trials are dominated by judges, rather than by lawyers. The judge investigates the facts of the case, interrogates the witnesses, passes judgement on the defendant and sentences him or her accordingly. Juries (made up of judges) are used only in the most important cases.

Opposite: **Two members of the police force. There are two police forces in Italy with general duties: the Pubblica Sicurezza, under the authority of the home secretary, and the Carabinieri, a corps of the armed forces under the minister of defense.**

LOCAL SYSTEMS OF GOVERNMENT

Italy is divided into 15 ordinary regions (Abruzzi, Puglia, Basilicata, Calabria, Campania, Emilia-Romagna, Lazio, Liguria, Lombardy, the Marches, Molise, Piedmont, Tuscany, Umbria and Veneto) and five special regions (Friuli-Venezia Giulia, Sicily, Sardinia, Valle d'Aosta and Trentino-Alto Adige). Regions are governed by regional councils that elect a president and the members of an executive committee. The special regions, populated by citizens of varying cultures, often with their own official languages, have more freedom than the ordinary regions to make legislative decisions.

Italy's 20 regions are further divided into some 94 provinces which are similarly governed by executive councils and council presidents as well as by a provincial governor. Italy's provinces are made up of more than 8,000 communes, run by municipal councils.

Italian citizens may vote in national, regional and local elections upon reaching the age of 21. The turnout for elections in Italy is very high, reaching more than 90% of the electorate for parliamentary elections.

THE POWER OF POLITICS

On the surface, Italy is as democratic a nation as any other Western power. Citizens have the freedom to choose their leaders in fair elections and the leaders in turn are supposed to act out the wishes of the voters. In actuality, Italian government is an extremely complicated system.

The Italian government is run by Italian political parties, each of which is allowed representation in Parliament. When voters go to the polls, they vote for parties rather than for individuals. If a voter desires to cast his or her ballot for a certain person, he or she must also vote for the other candidates within that same party. Voters only have the ability to elect members of Parliament. Elected members then get together and choose the prime minister and the members of the cabinet.

To do this, they often form coalition governments made up of members of several different parties (notably the Christian Democrats, the Communists, the Socialists, the Italian Socialist Movement, the Social Democratic Party, and the Republican and Liberal parties). Unusual as it may sound, most Italian governments last only 10 months in office. The country has had 50 governments since World War II!

The power of the political party in Italy is all-encompassing. Government jobs on the regional, provincial and communal levels in Italy are handed out according to political affiliation. This system, known as patronage, can be dangerous. In Italy it is likely that one's job, one's house and pension, and one's wife's operation and brother's contract and son's promotion, all depend on the local party secretary or some other party official. If one lives in a district run by the Christian Democrats, then it makes sense to join the party, take part in all its many social activities and make sure that the Christian Democrats stay in power, even if they prove to be incompetent.

The Italian way of government appears extremely unstable. However, it is not as volatile as it sounds. Although the present prime minister, Giulio Andreotti, has been in and out of office some seven times in recent years, his party, the Christian Democrats, has dominated Italy's coalition governments since 1945 (except for a period in the early 1980s when Bettino Craxi of the Italian Socialist Party was prime minister).

A Communist rally. The Italian Communist Party is the largest Communist party in Western Europe.

Italians believe wholeheartedly in democracy (and still fear takeover by a fascist leader like Mussolini) which is why they allow every party to have representation in Parliament. But because the Italian government is represented by so many small parties, there is often so much political infighting and bickering among those who hold office that important reforms are rarely made, and the prime minister is often forced to dissolve the cabinet and regroup. A recent dissolution of government, in March of 1991, came about because members of conflicting political parties could not agree on matters concerning Italy's enormous budget deficit, how to deal with the "war" against the Mafia, and, ironically, how to restructure Italy's government to ensure future stability.

ATTITUDES TOWARD GOVERNMENT

The Italian government has had a reputation for gross inefficiency for many decades. Lines at banks and social service agencies are said to be endless. Court cases take years and years to come to trial. Forms and applications for government services take years to be reviewed and problems often never get solved by government intervention. Somehow, this inefficiency does not bother Italians. This may be due partially to the fact that many Italians are used to bureaucratic red tape, but also because many have found ways to successfully get round it. Italians often rely on relatives or close family friends to get things done.

Many Italians have little respect for the institution of government. They neither trust government officials nor follow the laws they write. (A

THE MAFIA: ITALY'S OTHER "GOVERNMENT"

Since the 19th century, southern Italy—Sicily, Calabria and Campania—has been governed to a large extent by a non-official group of families called the Mafia. Originally, the Mafia was established to maintain law, order and dignity in the lawless, anything-goes regions of Sicily. Mafiosi resolved conflicts within the community because officials (many of them foreigners) were unable to provide effective government. The Mafia gained respect by using violence and intimidation tactics. Members were sworn to an internal code of silence which prevented them from telling on other members—their "brothers."

After Italy was unified, the Mafia helped politicians win votes in exchange for political favors. Southern Italians looked to the Mafia to protect them and even paid them a kind of tax for their services. Many thought the Mafia was a necessary and even a positive force within the community. Although Mussolini attempted to wipe out the Mafia by forcing members to leave the country, many returned after World War II and took up where they had left off.

In the 1970s, the Mafia modernized and began to shift its position from protector of the people to sophisticated entrepreneur. Today, the Mafia is responsible for much of the world's drug trafficking and subsequent money laundering. The organization provides the United States with most of its heroin, and Italy itself has more heroin addicts than any other nation in continental Europe. The Mafia has infiltrated the southern Italian government and also bought its way into legitimate corporations throughout the country. It is said to gross some $75 billion annually.

In the late 1970s and early 1980s, the Italian government made the brave decision to finally halt the horrendous activities of the Mafia. Spurred by the murders of anti-Mafia officials and their families, the government made it a crime to be a member of a Mafia organization. In 1987, 14 Mafia members broke the code of silence to provide incriminating evidence against hundreds of their brothers. Some 338 Mafiosi were convicted in what was considered the largest Mafia trial in Italian history. In 1988, however, the Mafia again began murdering government officials, including an important judge. This time Italians reacted with even tougher anti-Mafia laws and a stronger commitment to rid their country of the Mafia once and for all.

good number of Italians do not believe in paying income taxes.) Italians follow political events with a passion (politics in Italy are rarely boring), but they see the workings of government as a joke or a farce and the leaders as fools.

Perhaps many Italians pay little heed to authority because they are governed by other institutions such as the all-powerful family and the Catholic Church. The rules and regulations of government are not nearly as effective in keeping chaos at bay as the duty of a son to his mother or the sinner to the priest.

ECONOMY

ITALY IS AT ONCE a stunningly rich country and a shamefully poor one. A wealthy woman in the industrial north might spend her days shopping on Milan's fanciest streets, dressed more fashionably than her Parisian counterpart, while a female laborer in the underdeveloped south labors 10 hours a day in the dry, stingy soil of a small farm. Before World War II, however, many more Italians lived like the laborer than the well-dressed shopper. Then, Italy was among Europe's poorest countries, with a rich cultural legacy but a low standard of living.

The postwar years in Italy were a period of huge economic growth now commonly called the "economic miracle." Between 1945 and 1960, industries grew substantially in the north and southerners migrated to fill factory jobs. Technically advanced farm machinery replaced human labor and changed the country's economy from a primarily agricultural one to an industrial one. Income levels doubled and people began saving their money and investing it within the country. By the 1960s, unemployment had nearly disappeared. By the 1970s, Italy was ranked among the world's top seven industrial powers. Now it is ranked fifth—behind the United States, Japan, Germany and France, and ahead of Great Britain. Italians are Europe's largest savers (they save an average of 21% of their incomes) and have been called Europe's most adaptable, innovative entrepreneurs.

According to a recent survey, about 40% of Italian consumers today think of themselves as "rich and sophisticated." Italians currently spend 50% more on consumer goods such as clothing, automobiles and travel than they did in 1975. About two-thirds of the population own their own home and 25% of Italians have a second home. Today, it costs more to live in Rome than it does to live in New York.

Opposite: **Small shops lining a street of the cliffside town of Positano. With 50 million visitors a year, tourism is an important industry in Italy.**

33

FACTS AND FIGURES

In 1989, Italy had a Gross Domestic Product (GDP) of $865.8 billion, with an annual growth rate of 3.2%. The average per capita income that year was $15,052 and the average inflation rate had held steady at 5.5% since 1985. The growth rate has slowed a bit since the end of the 1980s, but the economy is still considered a healthy one.

The port of Brindisi. Italy being a country of meager natural resources, its exports consist almost entirely of manufactured goods and agricultural products.

The country's primary natural resources include natural gas and fish, while its major agricultural products are rice, grapes, olive oil, wheat and citrus fruits. Its major industrial products are automobiles, machinery, chemicals, textiles and shoes.

Exports in the year 1989 totaled $141.1 billion and were primarily made up of machinery and transport equipment, textiles, food products, chemicals and shoes. Imports, at $153.2 billion, were made up of the same products as well as petroleum, metals, cotton and wool. Italy's main trade partners were, in descending order of importance: Germany, France, the United States, Great Britain, OPEC (Organization of Petroleum Exporting Countries) and the Soviet Union.

The unemployment rate was 12% overall in 1989, but only 6% in the industrial north, 10% in the central regions, and about 20% in the south. Of the unemployed, approximately 70% were Italians under age 30.

SECTORS OF THE ECONOMY

AGRICULTURE Approximately 41% (or 30 million acres) of Italy's land are presently being farmed. Most farms are very small—about seven acres—and owned by individual families. About 10% of the labor force today hold jobs in agriculture, compared with 16% in 1974, and about 30% in 1963 and more than 50% before World War II.

Italy's most important agricultural crops are sugar beets, soybeans, wheat, corn, tomatoes, potatoes, oranges, lemons and limes. In the mid-1980s, Italy produced more than 6 million liters of wine (as much as France) and 537,000 tons of olive oil (most of it from the southern regions of Puglia and Calabria). Although Italy grows a large percentage of its own wheat, quantities must still be imported from other countries. Other imports include meat, live animals, corn (for animal feed) and tobacco.

Agriculture is still an important sector of the Italian economy, although Italy has moved from a primarily agricultural society to an industrial one.

MINING Italy produces significant amounts of iron ore, zinc, lead, pyrites, feldspar, mercury and coal, but is dependent on other countries for other minerals. Large quantities of natural gas are produced in the Po Valley but most of the country's supply is brought in from the Soviet Union. Unfortunately, Italy produces only about 20% of the petroleum it needs for domestic use. The government is trying to decrease the nation's use of crude oil in favor of coal and natural gas. Italians are generally against the use of nuclear power as a source of energy and recently voted down a government proposal to build more nuclear power plants.

Steel cutting in Milan, an important industrial city. The growth of Italy's industrial production in the postwar years is matched only by that of Japan and Germany (west).

INDUSTRY Italy is a land of a handful of large, powerful corporations—Fiat, the automobile company; Olivetti, the computer manufacturer; and Pirelli, the tire-maker, to name the top three—and great numbers of small, family-owned shops that produce top-quality goods. Italy has more small family establishments than other countries in Europe—one shop for every 67 people—and small businesses are considered the backbone of the economy. Italians like to keep their businesses small so the family can maintain control. Many of these industries have surprisingly advanced machinery and are able to deliver orders on a timely basis without sacrificing quality. If a very large order comes in, they often subcontract to fellow businesses in the area, as similar companies tend to gather in certain cities. Italian silk manufacturers, for instance, are concentrated in Como, makers of ceramics in Sassulo, and textile manufacturers in Prato, near Florence.

About one-third of the work force is employed in industry-related fields, including tourism, a service industry and an important sector of the economy. Most of the country's heavy industry is located in the Milan-Turin-Genoa triangle in the north. Major industrial products include: steel, pig iron, cement, household appliances, computers, automobiles, chemicals such as nitric acid, caustic soda and sulfuric acid, and textiles. Italy also has a large petroleum refining industry.

The fashion industry in Italy does not contribute as much money to the economy as the auto industry, for instance, but it has brought and continues to bring great distinction to the country. Italians themselves are extremely fashion-conscious and take great pride in their appearance. Italian designers have a special affinity for fabrics and are known for their bold experiments with innovative shapes and colors.

Milan is the fashion capital of Italy and, possibly, the world. Every October, thousands of fashion editors and clothing buyers from all over the world gather there to view the next season's collections. Milan is home to some of the world's most important designers and their studios: Krizia, famous for knits; Giorgio Armani, known in particular for exquisite menswear; Missoni, noted for beautifully crafted sweaters; Fendi, known for elegant leather goods; Ferragamo, the shoe manufacturer; Benetton, the famed color-conscious store for young people; Gucci, acclaimed for classically designed goods dotted with status-elevating "G"s.

Italian fashion is much sought after throughout the world.

Rush hour. Italians are generally hard working, but they manage to maintain a healthy balance between work and leisure and family.

Gianni Versace, possibly Italy's most famous designer, runs his business in a typically Italian fashion. His sister is his creative partner for the women's and children's collections; her husband is his right-hand man regarding the men's collections; and his brother is the firm's financial wizard. The Versaces were raised in Calabria, one of Italy's poorest areas.

Gianni came to Milan in the early 1970s when the city's fashion industry was just starting to make a name for itself. Today, he is known for his wildly patterned women's evening wear, his $700 men's silk shirts and the clothes he creates for rock stars Bruce Springsteen, Sting, Elton John, David Bowie, Phil Collins, Eric Clapton and Rod Stewart to wear on stage. He also designs costumes for operas and ballets, and his work has been exhibited in great museums. In 1990, his firm sold $615 million in wholesale figures. "I am the luckiest designer on earth," he said in a recent interview. "...I have my family."

THE ITALIAN WORK DAY

Italians have achieved economic success by working hard and by taking care in creating a good product. Nevertheless, they have always maintained

FOCUS ON FIAT

With $40 billion in annual sales, the Turin-based Fiat automobile company is Italy's largest corporation. Founded in 1899, Fiat stands for Fabbrica Italiana Automobili Torino. The Fiat Group, which includes Lancia, Alfa Romeo and Ferrari, sells more cars in both Italy and Europe than its closest competitors: Volkswagen, Peugeot, Ford, General Motors and all the Japanese manufacturers. The Fiat plants use

the most sophisticated robots in the world and their productivity rates are quite high.

The man who runs the Fiat "empire," as it is often called, is Gianni Agnelli, grandson of the founder and Italy's most powerful businessman. The 69-year-old Agnelli, Italy's richest citizen, is a source of endless fascination for the Italian public. Aside from Fiat, Agnelli also has financial interests in department stores, banks, publishing companies and tractor, truck and airplane manufacturers. He also owns one of Italy's best soccer teams, Juventus, and is personally responsible for about 5% of the nation's GDP.

a healthy balance between work and leisure. They are not likely to spend as much time at the office away from their families as many American business people. Fortunately, their families are often involved in their work and time off is often spent together.

A foreign visitor to Italy is often surprised by the fact that shops and businesses literally shut down for several hours in the middle of the day and stay open quite late into the evening. In the north, the average business is open from about 8:30 a.m. until 12:30 p.m., and then again from 3 p.m. until about 6 p.m. In the central and southern regions, businesses stay open from 9 a.m. to 1 p.m. and 4 p.m. to 8 p.m. Most shops stay open until 8 p.m. every evening. Banks and government offices are usually open only from about 8:30 a.m. until about 1:30 p.m. Restaurants are the only places open in the middle of the day.

A cobbler in Sorrento. Italy is a country of great economic differences, with a small group of people enjoying great wealth and a large part of the population living in varying degrees of poverty.

In general, Italians work a 5-day, 40-hour week. They have 10 paid holidays and two to four weeks of paid vacation, usually taken in August. Many people receive a bonus of one month's salary in December and a cost-of-living increase every quarter. Sometimes employers help pay for employees' housing and transportation costs; some even contribute money toward school fees for the children of employees.

Italian business people may enjoy their leisure time but they are hard workers. When they make an appointment with someone, they expect the meeting to begin on time. Often, the first few minutes of the session will be spent in non-business discussion, especially if the attendees are meeting for the first time. Family is a typical topic of conversation. People doing business together will often meet over lunch or dinner, and occasionally, at a nightclub.

ECONOMIC PROBLEMS

Although Italy has had an impressive postwar economic record, the economy is not without some serious problems. First of all, Italy has an enormous budget deficit: it is five times the size of the U.S. deficit and is equivalent to the country's GNP (the U.S. deficit is only half of its GNP). Much of the deficit problem has been blamed on the fact that Italians from all walks of life—small business people, professionals, laborers—do not pay income tax to the government. Many people have second jobs and neglect to report their additional income. Experts estimate that if the incomes made in what is called the "submerged

Sunning fruit in southern Italy. The agricultural south of Italy is much poorer than the industrial north.

economy" were reported, the country's GNP would increase by about 20%. Economists are hoping that some of Italy's deficit problems will start to iron themselves out in 1992, when the Economic Community (EC), of which Italy is a member, becomes a true common market with common economic policies which all member countries have to comply with.

There is also the problem of the economically disadvantaged south, an area that has often been likened to a third world country or an underdeveloped nation. The most disadvantaged regions in the south are said to be Calabria and Campania, and the poorest city Naples. Not only does the south suffer from a frighteningly high unemployment rate of 20%, but its illiteracy and birth rates are also higher than in the north. Predictably, income levels are considerably lower: the per capita income in Palermo, Sicily, is only half what it is in the northern city of Turin. In addition, many major corporations hesitate to locate in the southern regions because much of the area is controlled by the Mafia.

ITALIANS

WITH A POPULATION of approximately 57.5 million, Italy is among the most crowded nations in Europe. Rome is the most populous city, with about 3 million inhabitants, followed by Milan (1.5 million), Naples (1.2 million), Turin (1 million), Genoa (735,000), Palermo (720,000), Bologna (440,000) and Florence (430,000).

POPULATION FACTS AND FIGURES

About 70% of Italians live in urban areas. The nationwide population density is about 492 per square mile. The regions of Trentino-Alto Adige, Sardinia, Basilicata and Valle d'Aosta are the least dense—with only 168 people per square mile—while Lombardy, Campania and Liguria each has more than 780 people per square mile.

The average life expectancy for Italians is 73 years. The population appears to be aging. Only about 16% of Italians are under age 15. (In Turkey, the figure is 36%, while in the U.S., it is 22%.) The number of schoolchildren dropped from 10.7 million in 1985 to 9.5 million in 1989.

Despite the fact that Italy is a predominantly Roman Catholic country, the national fertility rate is among the world's lowest, with women having an average of only 1.3 children. At this rate, experts say, the population of Italy will decline to under 56 million by the year 2020. Italian women are electing to work rather than to have large families, and they have recognized how difficult it is to raise children in a society with little adequate day care and a steadily increasing cost of living. Women living in the northern regions of Friuli-Venezia Giulia, Liguria, Emilia-Romagna, Valle d'Aosta and Tuscany tend to have fewer babies than the national average, while women in the southern areas of Sicily, Campania, Puglia and Calabria tend to have more. Similarly, the infant mortality rate in the north is lower than that in the south.

Opposite: Italian lass. The Italian nation is a relatively recent creation. Italians gained independence and unity only in the 19th century. This perhaps explains why Italians tend to identify more with the region they come from than with the country.

RACE AND ETHNIC GROUPS

Italians living in the northern regions of the country are difficult to distinguish from other northern Europeans due to various invasions by Germanic, French and Slavic people that took place over many centuries. Northern Italians generally look like German and French people, although there are fewer blonds in Italy, except in the Alpine regions and in parts of the Po Valley and the region of Tuscany. Inhabitants of southern Italy, colonized by the Greeks in ancient times, have a distinctly Mediterranean look: dark skin tone, brown eyes and brown hair. Northern Italians are said to be slightly taller than southern Italians.

Enjoying a beer— German-Italians in South Tyrol.

There are smaller numbers of Italians of German, French, Slavic, Greek and Albanian heritage living in various regions of the country. German-Italians presently total approximately 0.25% of the population. In addition, there are presently large numbers of immigrants (many illegal) from such places as Ethiopia, Albania, Yugoslavia, the Philippines, Poland and North Africa living and working within the country's borders. Most immigrants come to the large cities to do menial, labor-intensive jobs. They generally congregate in certain sectors of the city and establish their own neighborhoods and shops. Some officials estimate that the immigrant population now exceeds 1 million or about 2% of the population. The bigger cities in Italy also attract large numbers of gypsy families (who are mostly of Eastern European origin), but their numbers are difficult to calculate.

MIGRATION

One factor that profoundly affected Italy's population patterns in the past was migration by Italians to other nations, and more recently, by southern Italians to areas of northern Italy.

From 1861 to 1973 (when migration began to ease), some 26 million Italians left the country of their birth. From 1850 to 1880, some 120,000 Italians left Italy each year; by 1913, the figure was close to a million. Many of the Italians who left their homeland around the turn of the century were from the south.

Among other places, they migrated to the United States, where they made a significant impact on the culture they found there. Between 1876 and 1910, in fact, about 6 million Italians went to the United States. By 1922, the U.S. immigration department disallowed entry to Italians, so many of them settled within Europe. Between 1946 and 1973, some 7.1 million Italians made their homes in countries such as Germany, France and Switzerland, but about 4 million of them returned to Italy. It was not until 1973 that these massive migration patterns began to reverse themselves and more Italians returned home than left.

Today, with Italy's prosperity, people need not leave the country to find work. Many southern Italians, however, feel the need to move north, especially to Rome and the industrial triangle formed by Milan, Turin and Genoa, in search of employment and a better quality of life.

"In the heart of every man, wherever he is born, whatever his education and tastes, there is one small corner which is Italian, that part which finds regimentation irksome, the dangers of war frightening, strict morality stifling, that part which loves frivolous and entertaining art, admires larger-than-life-size solitary heroes, and dreams of an impossible liberation from the strictures of a tidy existence."

—from The Italians *by Luigi Barzini*

THE ITALIAN CHARACTER

Although the general character of a nation as large as Italy is difficult to pinpoint, there are some basic traits that accurately describe the Italian personality, at least on the surface. Visitors to Italy (40 to 50 million people each year) notice right away the openness and gregariousness of the Italian people.

They seem to have a love of life and to enjoy life's pleasures to the fullest. Looking good is quite important to them and they tend to have an almost natural ability to appear stylish. Italians admire people who are cosmopolitan, but who also have a respect for tradition. Italians have a deep respect for the arts, and creativity is encouraged in both sexes at an early age.

They are an emotional people and are generally less haughty and stiff than some of their European neighbors. They have a pointed dislike for authority, yet seem to accept inefficiency in their government with little complaint. They are highly individualistic yet they respect the institution of the family and are dutiful sons and daughters, mothers and fathers.

REGIONALISM

Italians probably identify more strongly with their regions than with the nation that unifies them. And, people from different regions are associated with different personality traits. The Milanese are said to be more business-minded, less warm and more sophisticated than other Italians. Piedmontese are supposed to be prouder and more reserved than people from other regions. Neapolitans have a reputation for being very easy going. Florentines love to try new things, but they continue to revere their Renaissance past. Romans are supposed to be combative, Venetians passive.

If any animosity exists among Italians from different areas, it is strongest between Italians from the north and those from the south. The "north" of Italy is the area from the Adriatic port of Ancona to the southern part of Rome. The "south" is the regions below this line (called the "Ancona Wall" by Italians). The south is referred to in Italy as the Mezzogiorno ("mayd-dzo-JOR-no"), which means "land of the midday sun." The south makes up about 40% of the country's land but is home to 35% of its people who contribute only 24% of its GDP. The division between the north and the south is so strong in Italy that President Francesco Cossiga likened it to an invisible Berlin Wall. "Materially and morally, the iron curtain runs through our own people," he said.

Sardinian woman. The prosperous and progressive northerners look down on their impoverished and backward southern compatriots.

Schoolboys on an outing. Public facilities such as schools and hospitals are said to be better in the north than in the south.

Northern Italians feel they are more sophisticated than southern Italians. Most of the country's industry is in the north as well as the nation's most vital cities. The south is primarily agricultural, on the other hand, and therefore "backward," according to many northerners. Hospitals, schools, communication and transportation systems and government services in the north are said to be better than those in the south and, as of 1990, southerners were considerably poorer than northerners. The unemployment rate in the north was about 8%, while in the south it stood at 20%; and the typical southerner made only 56% of the salary of the northerner.

Since World War II, the Italian government has spent about $300 billion in an effort to help the people of the south, but the economic and social gaps between the two regions continue to widen. Northerners resent the government's focus on the south and what they consider to be its misuse of taxpayers' money. They feel that the money goes straight into the corrupt hands of the Mafia that dominates the south. Southerners, on the contrary, feel that the north has long meddled in its affairs without making much progress.

CLASS DISTINCTIONS

Social classes exist in Italy, but there is more mobility between classes than in other Western European nations. General class distinctions are made between people who live in urban areas and those who live in rural areas; those in the north versus those in the south; those who run or own large corporations versus those who have small family businesses; people with large agricultural holdings versus small farmers; skilled workers versus unskilled workers.

A blue-collar worker. While in the past, one's social status was determined by wealth, family history and family connections, today it is increasingly being measured by merit and education.

Some social scientists divide Italy's social system into the following groups: the elite or governing class, the middle class, the urban proletariat and the rural class. The elite class (about 10% of the population) is made up of those with the best education, the nation's intellectuals and professionals. It also includes wealthy people in business and the landowning aristocracy. The middle class (about 35% of the population) is made up of people with some education and defined job skills: white-collar workers, artisans and small businessmen. The urban proletariat (35%) is the less educated, but stable, working class, and the rural class (20%) consists of small landowners and the tenants and day laborers who farm the land. Some of those who belong to this last category hold additional part-time jobs. Others are migrant farmers who travel from region to region finding work where they can.

LIFESTYLE

MOST ITALIANS DWELL IN urban areas where space is limited, so they generally live in multi-story apartment houses.

APARTMENT LIVING

The typical apartment building is made of cement or stone; the average unit is about 1,000 square feet in total area and has all the modern conveniences. Adequate, affordable housing for the poor and middle class is difficult to find in larger cities such as Milan, Rome and Naples. The poor must often resort to living in shanties on the outskirts of the city until they can afford decent housing.

Even those who can afford good housing in Rome often have difficulty finding it. Like New York, rents in Rome are exorbitant, and what an apartment rents for is not necessarily what it is worth. Unfurnished apartments come without "furnishings" of any kind: no closets, no lights, no kitchen appliances and sometimes no water heaters. Much of the plumbing in the older buildings is unreliable and the elevators are often out of order. (Like pay toilets, some elevators require that the rider insert a coin before the door opens.) Electricity is expensive so central heating is often turned on as late as possible in the season and only during certain hours—from 8 to 10 in the morning and from 5 to 9 in the evening is typical.

Opposite and above: **Apartment living is a way of life in Italy's cities.**

An old Italian villa in Rome.

In the typical American city, shops and businesses are segregated from residential areas; in Italy's large metropolises they mingle together naturally. In cities like New York and Chicago, downtown areas often empty out after 5 p.m. This doesn't happen in most Italian cities because many large buildings are broken up into storefronts that face the street and apartments that face the interior courtyard. Restaurants and gathering places like cafés can be found on almost every block, so the streets have a lively, social atmosphere nearly every hour of the day and night.

ITALIAN HOUSES

The typical Italian house is a two-story dwelling made of brick or stone. The roofs are often tiled and the property usually includes some kind of enclosed yard. Poorer people often live in small, two-room dwellings.

The old Italian villas still seen today in both rural and urban areas often have elaborate columns and are built around several interior courtyards. In the country, the ground floor might be used for farm equipment, while in the city, it functions as a shop, garage or office. The second floor is often where the family lives, and higher storys, if they exist, might be used as reception areas or guest bedrooms. Many of the older houses in large cities might look rather dirty and shabby on the outside (with a few elegant architectural details), but they are often magnificent on the inside. The courtyards are quiet and peaceful and the rooms that look out onto them have marble floors and 12-foot ceilings. Some are decorated with antiques, others with sleek, modern furniture of Italian design. Even in the smallest homes much thought is put into interior decor, as Italians care very much about the way things look.

Many upper-class Italian families have country homes that they use for weekend or holiday getaways. Some are estates that have been passed down from generation to generation; others are old farmhouses that have been renovated for modern living.

THE NOTION OF BELLA FIGURA

Italians are very conscious of their appearance and have been for centuries. Appearance, to Italians, is as important as, and sometimes more important than, reality. The Italian notion of looking good and showing a confident, competent face to the world is known as *bella figura*. Displaying *la bella figura* is important to Italians of all social classes, to people from both the cosmopolitan north and the less developed south. The wealthy Milanese might possess the means to achieve a good appearance more than the Neapolitan, but both manage to appear stylish, even if it means not having enough money for more life-sustaining things.

"[Italians] judge men and events less by what they read or learn, and far more by what they see, hear, touch and smell."
—*Luigi Barzini,*
The Italians.

53

Italians, though highly individualistic, are social beings. Because they so often find themselves in the company of others, they feel that they owe it to their companions to look nice—consistently. They desire both to give pleasure and to receive it; and they adore both giving compliments and receiving them. Men often wear the most fashionable silk ties, knotted tightly, with exquisitely cut Italian suits; women have the finest leather shoes, highly polished, and the most elegant blouses and skirts, pressed to perfection. Italians, though good wine drinkers, do not let themselves get drunk—this would make them appear slovenly and out of control.

The typical Italian never wears shorts in a large city. Jeans are commonly worn, but not if they are torn or frayed. Casual attire is often of high quality. Both men and women wear stylish Italian suits to work. When they attend a play or an opera, Italian men wear classic suits and ties, and women wear fancy dresses with high heels. Black tie attire is appropriate for opening nights at the famous opera houses. Many women wear hats and dresses with long sleeves to church.

This feeling of wanting to be beautiful extends to villages or towns, especially on an important feast day when visitors from other areas come to share in the festivities. Even cars are kept impeccably clean.

Promenading in San Remo. Young or old, poor or rich, the Italian takes great care in his or her appearance.

INSTITUTIONAL INEFFICIENCY

Although Italians care very much for creating the impression of individual competence, this feeling does not extend to Italian institutions. The Italian government, its postal service, telephone company, transportation system, hospitals and schools are notoriously inefficient and badly managed. Italians are very much aware of the fact that their country does not run as smoothly as say England, Germany or the United States, but they have traditionally had little feeling for the welfare of the group as opposed to the family or the individual. They trust themselves and their families, but not the impersonal organization.

Gross incompetence on the part of institutions and bureaucracies hinders the everyday lives of most Italians. Letters sent within the country, for instance, take at least seven days to reach their destination. Italian checks take six days to clear, while foreign ones take 15. Trains and buses rarely run on time and appalling traffic jams and their accompanying pollution plague all the major cities. Having an operation in an Italian hospital can be a nightmare due to terrible overcrowding. (In the south, some patients have to rely on relatives to bring them their meals.) Government offices are said to be full of stacks and stacks of forms that have been filled out but never processed, while modern computers sit quietly because nobody has learned how to use them.

Italy's telephone system has many critics. Phone numbers can be four, five, six, seven or eight digits, and only about 52% of calls get through the first time the numbers are dialed. Many times, the caller gets a frustrating busy signal when he enters the first digit; other times he gets through only to realize he has a crossed line and must persuade the other party to hang up so he can talk. (This does not often work.) Getting a new phone installed can take up to a year.

THE PATRONAGE SYSTEM

Part of the reason why Italy's public services are so inefficient is because the country's civil servants are hired according to who they know and not what they know. They are also employed for life and therefore have no fears that incompetence will lead to their getting fired. Most of Italy's government employees get their jobs because they belong to the same political party that the person hiring does. In other words, the head of a department, a member of the Christian Democrats for instance, will hire another Christian Democrat in return for a vote in the next election. The voter might not believe in the political stance of the candidate, but he votes for him anyway because he has received a favor and must do what he can to repay it. Obviously, this leads neither to meaningful change within the ministries of the civil service nor within the political system. This procedure is known as patronage and is widely practiced in Italy, a country with more than 2 million civil servants or 18% of the work force—most of them southerners.

Government jobs in Italy may be secure, but they do not necessarily pay well. Therefore, many government employees take second or even third jobs to supplement their incomes. According to a recent study, more than half of Italy's civil servants have second jobs and of these 33% sell goods to other civil servants while on the job and 27% actually even manage another business during office hours. Some people even leave their first jobs after lunch to report to their second jobs without being reprimanded.

THE IMPORTANCE OF THE FAMILY

Italians may not be loyal to government officials or to the nation as a whole, but they are true devotees to the institution of the family. The individual may matter a great deal in Italy, but not at the expense of the family. Italians believe the family name is all important and should not be tarnished by the thoughtless acts of one family member. Pride in the family and the upholding of solid family values has probably been responsible for keeping the country together and allowing it to prosper, despite its economic, social and political problems.

Italians spend more time together as a family than most other people from Western cultures. Even when the children grow up, they often elect to live with their parents until they get married. Then, they join the family business, set up house near their parents, eat with them, visit them and travel with them. More aged parents live with their children than in the United States, and many Italians feel it their duty to care for their parents themselves rather than place them in a nursing home. Grandparents help make important domestic decisions and often take care of the young children in the house while the mothers go to work.

In the northern, highly industrialized areas of Italy, the power of the family seems to be lessening as the society becomes wealthier and the cost of living goes up. Many inhabitants of expensive, crowded cities such as Rome and Milan can only afford small houses—without extra rooms for their parents. Many of Rome's elderly, it seems, are now finding themselves alone, without the support system of the family to care for them, and without the finances to live in a private rest home.

Furthermore, the nuclear Italian family is getting smaller. As with many American women, Italian women today often feel the need to take a job outside the home to help supplement the family income, and this often leads to the decision to have fewer babies. Northern Italy, in fact, has a significantly lower birth rate than southern Italy, and the growth rate for the country as a whole ranks among the lowest in Western Europe.

A wedding reception. The family is of great importance to the Italian. Children often live at home until they get married. After marriage, many try to set up house near their parents.

57

Italians indulge their children to the extent of spoiling them.

ITALIAN CHILDREN

Italians may be having smaller families, but they remain unconditionally devoted to their children. Italian babies and toddlers are heavily indulged. They are permitted to do as they please and are rarely disciplined for being loud or for running wild in public places; they are seldom spanked for misbehaving. Italian parents are very affectionate toward their children and have no inhibitions about hugging and kissing them in front of others. They will even reach out to touch strangers' children if they think they are beautiful. Children are equal members of the household in Italy; they are allowed to express their opinions and are treated as individuals. Italian children seem very comfortable with their parents and, when they grow up, they readily admit that they truly like them.

Italian parents are ambitious and self-sacrificing for their children without being pushy. Unlike some American parents, Italian parents are less likely to encourage their children to learn to read or to play an instrument at a young age. They tend to feel that children will learn these skills all in good time and that they should not have the pressure to achieve thrust upon them before they are ready. Italian parents want their children to have what they did not and tend to spoil them. Parents delight in holding elaborate parties for their children's birthdays and for the most important day in the child's life, the First Communion. If possible, large numbers of guests will be invited to a celebration dinner and the child will receive a present from each one.

Historically, male children have been preferred to female children in Italy, although this appears to be changing. Boys are treated like royalty within the household: they are rarely criticized, much of their behavior goes unsupervised, and their every whim is gratified. Above all, they are able to carry on the family name. Girls, on the other hand, are watched more carefully and tend to be molded into demure, but strong, self-sacrificing women.

Making *tortellini* at home. Traditionally, women were expected to stay at home after marriage to take care of house and children. This is changing as more women are choosing to continue working outside the home after marriage.

SEX ROLES

In Italy, the father is very much the head of the household and the children give him the respect he is due. He rules by authority and tends to keep his distance from the children. Italian men flaunt their masculinity and, on the whole, are not as willing to participate in domestic chores—like cleaning house or taking care of the children—as men from other cultures. Traditional Italian men see themselves as the protectors of the females in the household. Their wives, daughters and mothers have a Madonna-like virtue and innocence, and their honor must be upheld.

Italian women are said to be less militant about their feminism than American women. They cultivate femininity in their appearance, and many of those who work a full day still return home to perform all the domestic functions of a non-working woman.

Many conservative Italian men see women as *angelo del focolare* ("AHN-jay-lo del fo-ko-LAA-ray") or "angels of the hearth"—which means that they are responsible for church, children and kitchen.

Italian mothers are great nurturers and provide warmth and affection to all the members of the family. Although outwardly it may appear that the mother is subordinate to the father, she is often the true head of the household. She makes sure the children are properly dressed, that they learn good manners and that they know the difference between right and wrong. She also provides the meals for the family—a very important task in a food-worshiping culture like Italy's.

The mother-son relationship in Italy is said to be the strongest familial tie and sons often revere their mothers over their fathers, and later, over their own children and wives. As a child, the son is the mother's true pride and joy, and as an adult, she will continue to give him any care and attention he needs.

FEMINISM AND WOMEN'S RIGHTS

Italy underwent a feminist revolution in the 1970s when women aggressively sought equal rights with men under the law. Up until the late 1960s, it was a crime in Italy for a woman—but not a man—to have an extramarital affair, and both abortion and divorce were illegal. It was legal for a man to kill another man if he sexually harmed or had an affair with his wife, sister or daughter. Women were often treated as subordinates by males; wives were not encouraged to work outside the home and their lives were completely focused on pleasing their husbands and children. Many women were illiterate because their families never felt it necessary to send them to school.

In 1970, divorce was legalized in Italy and women were ensured the

More and more women are working at jobs which were traditionally the domain of men.

rights to receive alimony and child support payments from their former husbands. Despite many people's fears, once divorce was legalized, marriages did not dissolve at a significantly higher rate. In fact, in Italy, the divorce rate is much lower than in Sweden, France and Great Britain. In the late 70s, abortion was legalized in Italy—a surprising decision for a country dominated by Catholics. Today, Italian women can even receive government funds to obtain an abortion.

Women in Italy received equal rights in the workplace in 1977. This law ensures that women are paid on par with men when performing similar jobs. When Italian women leave their jobs to have children, they are given five months' paid leave, another six months of unpaid leave and the guarantee that they can have the same job when they return.

Before World War II, few Italian women were employed outside the home or the farm. As in many Western nations, most women in Italy today need to work to help support the family. Now, Italy has significant proportions of women lawyers, professors, members of Parliament and business managers. Approximately 25% of doctors and 40% of the Fiat work force are women.

The University of Bologna, established in the 11th century, is the oldest in Italy and all of Europe. Many Italian universities are extremely overcrowded; the University of Rome, for instance, has more than 160,000 students. Most programs take four years to complete. Advanced degrees in architecture and medicine take five and six years, respectively.

EDUCATION

School in Italy is compulsory for children from age 6 to 14. Both public institutions and private schools are controlled by the government's ministry of education and their curriculum is similar. Three- and four-year-olds can attend a special day school if their mothers work, but this is not mandatory. Five-year-olds go to kindergarten, and children 6 through 10 to elementary school where they study subjects such as reading, math, history, science, art and music. Many elementary schools have half-day programs that the child attends six days a week.

In middle school, children aged 11–13 take up the same subjects, but they also learn a second language. At 14, children can elect to discontinue their education or go on to a five-year upper secondary school where they specialize in either vocational or teacher training or prepare for a university education. Fields of study in vocational schools include agriculture, business and aeronautics, while common subjects in the academic program are literature, science, Latin, Greek, philosophy, fine arts and history. Most middle- and upper-class children opt for the academic rather than the vocational program.

Italian students are expected to study diligently and they face difficult

TIDBITS ABOUT THE ITALIAN WAY OF LIFE

The people of Italy have certain customs, ways of living, social do's and don'ts, oddities and characteristics that both illuminate their character and distinguish them from others. Here are a few:

- Italians love to smoke and do not consider it a health hazard.
- Italians dislike drafts and air conditioning because they think these can cause sickness.
- Jogging is not a fad in Italy because Italians feel it is too physically strenuous.
- Milanese wear dark colors all year round; they always dress up and think shorts are only appropriate on the soccer field.
- Italians like to show affection (of the amorous type) in public.
- Italians eat white food like rice, mozzarella cheese and potatoes when they are ill, to clear out the system.
- Italians who have just met rarely discuss their jobs; they prefer to talk about their families, good restaurants or soccer.
- Italians bargain for the goods they buy in most small shops or at open markets.
- Italy has no official drinking age and alcoholic beverages are served all day and all night at restaurants and bars.
- There is no official speed limit on Italian expressways.
- Italians drive very fast, with little worry of getting in an accident, and very aggressively, changing lanes and going through red lights at whim. Italians with sports cars are said to drive at 120 miles per hour on the highway.

examinations at regular intervals. University admission is guaranteed once a student graduates from secondary school. To graduate, a student must pass a two-day oral and written examination. There are 60 universities in Italy.

RELIGION

ANCIENT ROMAN BELIEFS

The ancient Romans worshiped many gods, goddesses and spirits, each of whom was responsible for a different feature of life. Juno was the goddess of women; Jupiter, the king of the gods, was the god of the sky; Mercury was the god of merchants; Vulcan the god of fire; Mars the god of war; Minerva the goddess of wisdom and handicrafts; Venus the goddess of fertility and love; Mithras the god of soldiers, etc. Gods and goddesses from other cultures were adopted by the ancient Romans as well: Bacchus or Dionysus, the Greek god of wine; Cybele, the Turkish goddess of motherhood; and Isis, from the Egyptian pantheon, who was concerned with reincarnation. Emperors and empresses were sometimes worshiped as gods after their deaths.

Emperors showed their devotion to their favored deities by building temples to them. Roman citizens left offerings such as food, milk, wine, money, jewels or statues at temple altars and engaged in ceremonies and animal sacrifices to win the gods' approval.

Opposite: **About 99% of the Italian population today are Roman Catholic, but the Church is becoming less important in the people's everyday life.**

65

ROME _ LE TIBRE

The river god, holding an oar in one of his arms. The ancient Romans worshiped many gods and goddesses and spirits.

The Romans were generally accepting of other people's religion but persecuted the Christians because, among other things, they displeased the gods by refusing to participate in such offerings. Christianity finally became the official religion during the 4th century.

ROMAN CATHOLICISM IN ITALY

Italy is a Roman Catholic country. Between the collapse of the Roman Empire and the year 1870, when Italy's varied regions were consolidated into one country with a central government, Roman Catholicism was its strongest unifying force. The popes who ruled the Catholic Church had tremendous influence—both political and spiritual—over Italy during the centuries before unification. The Vatican, the home of the pope and the center of the Roman Catholic world and its 800 million followers, is located within the city of Rome, although it is a separate sovereign state. In 1929, Roman Catholicism was made the state religion of Italy. Religious instruction in state schools was mandatory and the Church had the legal right to decide if films, books and theater productions were appropriate for Roman Catholic audiences or if they should be excluded because

they went against Catholic doctrine or showed the Church in an unfavorable light. In 1984, the church/state relationship in Italy was formally severed in an official concordat, although the document reaffirmed the Church's importance in the moral lives of Italians.

Today, approximately 99% of Italy's population are Roman Catholic, although, with the country's post-World War II "economic miracle" and the urbanization and prosperity of the average Italian, religion has become less and less a part of everyday life. Over the last several decades, Italians have decided that they wish to make decisions for themselves instead of dutifully adhering to the laws of the Church. Parishes are now so large in the cities that people no longer attend church simply because their neighbors will notice if they don't come. With fewer people working on the land, the fertility of which people traditionally felt could be affected by their devotion to God and the Church, people no longer "need" the Church as they once did.

"...whether he goes to church or not, Catholicism is still part of the Italian's psyche in the same way as lungs or a kidney are part of his body..."
—Italian Labyrinth
by John Haycraft

Laws legalizing abortion and divorce—both forbidden by the Catholic Church—were passed in the 1970s. Birth control, frowned upon by the Church, is widely practiced, as evidenced by the nation's declining birth rate. In 1985 a survey found that close to half of all Italians did not consider religion a meaningful part of their lives, and almost three-quarters of the population did not think the Church should have anything to do with the country's political system. (The Catholic Church and its followers had traditionally supported the Christian Democratic Party.)

Today, only about 25% of Italians attend church on a regular basis, compared to about 66% in the 1940s and 50s. Among those under age 35, about 17% go to church. Only about 6% of Catholics take communion regularly, and 30% go through the formal rite of receiving the sacraments before they die. The people who attend church today are generally very young children, women, the elderly and those living in the country, particularly in the south. Young men living in urban areas are the most infrequent churchgoers. Many of those who do go to church are farmers, technicians, craftsmen and clerks. Members of the upper class and the lower class do not attend Sunday Mass as often as members of the middle class.

These statistics, however, do not tell the whole story. Although most Italians are not regular churchgoers, many of them place more faith and trust in the Church than they do in the Italian government. Moreover, a great majority of Italians still turn to the Catholic Church to direct and perform the important moments, or rites of passage, in their lives: 99% of Roman Catholics are baptized in the Church; about 95% of children take First Communion; 82% are confirmed; and nearly 100% have Catholic weddings. Even members of the Italian Communist Party, which does not encourage religious ties, often participate in these Catholic rituals.

A ceiling fresco by Raphael, in the Vatican. Some of the world's finest works of art are inspired by the Roman Catholic religion.

The Roman Catholic Church also provides an enormous sense of pride for the Italian. As the home of Roman Catholicism, the Vatican is an immensely important institution. It contains some of the world's finest art, several significant universities and the actual home of the pope, whom Catholics consider the holiest man on earth. Many of Italy's Catholic churches—St. Peter's in the Vatican, especially—are architectural masterpieces and draw millions of visitors every year.

Most importantly, the Church in Italy sets a moral example for Italians. Whether or not the Italian of the 1990s follows the doctrines of the Church in their strictest sense, the Catholic Church is partially responsible for making him or her aware of the difference between right and wrong, and the importance of treating the needy with compassion. In fact, in Italy today, the Catholic Church's primary responsibility is helping people who are in trouble. It provides health and welfare services to the needy, runs programs for prostitutes, the elderly and people addicted to drugs, as well as homes for handicapped children and the mentally ill. It also provides employment aid for people who are out of work, food shelters for the hungry and, of course, religious education for young children.

The famed Swiss Guards of the Vatican City.

THE VATICAN CITY

The Vatican City State was given its sovereignty in 1929 by an agreement between Benito Mussolini's government and Pope Pius XI called the Lateran Treaty. Although the Vatican City takes up less than 109 acres (about the size of Central Park in New York City), it is really a fully functioning miniature country that happens to exist within the boundaries of the vast city of Rome. The most important structure within the Vatican boundaries is St. Peter's Basilica, the world's largest church. The Vatican also has its own prison, newspaper, army, the brilliantly costumed Swiss Guards (trained in karate since the assassination attempt on the pope in 1981), stamps, radio station (which makes international broadcasts in 35 different languages), a 1-million volume library, and the prestigious Pontifical Academy of Sciences, filled with many Nobel Prize winners.

The Vatican is probably most famous for its stunning art treasures. Ornate sculptures of the saints by 17th-century artist Gian Lorenzo Bernini

HOW TO ADDRESS THE POPE

When Italians see the pope during his weekly presentation to the public in the piazza of St. Peter, they shout, *"Viva il Papa!"* ("VEE-vah eel PAA-pah") or "Long live the Pope!" When meeting the pope in person, it is appropriate to call him either "Santissimo Padre" ("sahn-TEE-see-moh PAH-dray"), which means "Holy Father," or "Sua Santità" ("SOO-ah sahn-tee-tah"), which means "Your Holiness." Whereas former popes allowed followers to kiss their ring upon making their acquaintance, the present pope frowns upon such expressions of devotion.

The pope's official title, which might prove difficult to either shout out in a crowd or recite in person is, according to the Vatican directory: Bishop of Rome, Vicar of Jesus Christ, Successor of the Prince of the Apostles, Supreme Pontiff of the Universal Church, Patriarch of the West, Primate of Italy, Archbishop and Metropolitan of the Roman Province, Sovereign of the State of Vatican City, Servant of the servants of God. Italians, when talking among themselves, call him Papa Wojtyla or simply "this pope" as if they are aware of the fact that 263 popes came before him and many will surely follow. (Picture above shows a papal mass in the Vatican.)

sit atop the giant "arms" that encircle the beautiful piazza of St. Peter's. Michelangelo's magnificent *Pietà*, the *Apollo Belvedere* sculpture, and Raphael's fresco *The Liberation of St. Peter* are among the works in the Vatican museums, while Michelangelo's famous frescoes—which took nine years in all to paint—cover the ceiling of the Sistine Chapel, where the cardinals meet to elect a new pope.

Some 300 people—cardinals, altar boys, students and Swiss Guardsmen—are permanent residents of the Vatican, but the most important is the former Karol Cardinal Wojtyla, Pope John Paul II, the first Polish pope ever and the first non-Italian pope since 1523. He is known for his gentleness, his sincerity and his effort to unite the Catholics of the world through his international travel.

The interior of a synagogue in Florence. The Jews of Italy have traditionally been well assimilated into the local population. During World War II, Italians were protective of the Jews; they were not afraid to offer them hiding places from the Nazis and, as a result, fewer Italian Jews were sent to concentration camps than in neighboring European countries.

OTHER RELIGIONS

Only about 1% of Italians belong to religions other than Roman Catholicism. Moslems, mostly students and immigrants from Hungary, Albania, Bulgaria and Yugoslavia, make up one group. Many of Italy's Protestants belong to the Waldensian Church, started by Peter Waldo in the 12th century in southern France and northern Italy as a reaction against the Roman Catholic Church.

Jews make up the other significant non-Catholic group in Italy. Some descend from families who lived in Rome as far back as the pre-Christian era, others came from Spain in the 15th century and still others from Germany and Poland in the late 19th and early 20th centuries. Most of the Jewish community is centered in Milan and Rome, while Florence and

THE LEGEND OF ROMULUS AND REMUS

According to ancient Roman legend, Rome was founded in the year 753 B.C. by Romulus who, with his twin brother Remus, was left to die near the Tiber River by a wicked relative. The twins' mother was supposed to be the virgin Princess Rhea Silvia, who had been raped by Mars, the god of war. The brothers were saved by a she-wolf, who allowed them to suckle her for food, and raised by a herdsman. As an adult, Romulus decided to build a city on the spot where he had been saved and brought up. According to ancient Roman writings, Romulus marked out the four corners of the city, plowed a ditch from corner to corner to delineate the city boundaries and built a wall to fortify the area.

In 1990, Andrea Carandini, an Italian archeologist, set out to prove that the myth of Rome's founding was based on truth. By digging 20 feet under the Palatine, Carandini uncovered the wall he believed to be the one erected by Romulus. Nearby, he found pottery dating back to about 730 B.C., further evidence that Rome was founded during the time of Romulus. Unfortunately, Carandini has had to discontinue his search due to lack of government financing for the project, a common problem among archeologists in treasure-rich Italy.

Trieste have small congregations. An old Jewish neighborhood—synagogues and kosher restaurant intact—still survives in Rome.

Many Roman Catholics in Italy, particularly in the southern regions, still practice folk beliefs. Certain women in small villages are said to have magic powers. They are consulted for predictions about the future, for potions or charms to win lovers, or for favorable lottery numbers. Some southerners fear witches and actually perform animal sacrifices to keep witches away.

LANGUAGE

ITALIAN, THE NATIONAL LANGUAGE OF ITALY, is a Romance language descended from Vulgar Latin, the dialect spoken by the people living in the last years of the Roman Empire. Italian has more Latin words than the other Romance languages, such as Spanish and French, and its grammatical system is similar to that used in Latin. Latin is still the language of the Vatican City in Rome. Official papal documents are printed in Latin (as well as seven other languages).

Italian is supposed to be one of the most melodic, most expressive languages in the world. Italians use their language eloquently and dramatically, but they do not demand that foreigners speak it as well as they do. Italian is spoken by more than 60 million people in Italy, Switzerland, the United States, Canada, Argentina and Brazil.

REGIONAL DIALECTS

There are many regional dialects in Italy—Tuscan, Venetian, Piedmontese, to name a few. On the island of Sardinia alone there are four different dialects. When considering the Italian language, it is important to understand the difference between accent and dialect. In the United States or England, people who come from different regions and have different accents are likely to be able to understand one another. In Italy, however, some dialects are so drastically different that someone speaking one dialect may be unintelligible to someone from another region. In England, accents have direct correlation with social class; not so with dialects in Italy. In the mid-1980s, the vast majority (98%) of Italians were able to communicate in dialect. Many young people speak dialect at home, to their parents and grandparents, but standard Italian when outside the home. Dialect is still the primary means of communication in small agricultural towns or villages, or on small islands.

Opposite: **The Italian used in newspapers, business, radio and television is the dialect of Tuscany.**

One reason why dialects are so varied in Italy is because the country came to political unity so recently. In addition, Italy's unique geography isolated one region—and therefore one culture—from another, allowing each to flourish on its own. Many dialects were influenced by the language of neighboring countries, or by the language of invaders who at one time or another laid claim to the land.

Although most dialects have Latin roots, Aostan dialect is said to sound more like French than Italian. Venetian is sprinkled with Spanish and Portuguese words, and Piedmontese has a good deal of German

Dialects are still spoken among old people in the countryside, but among the younger generation they are fading away.

mixed in. Southern Italian dialects have a Greek influence. Fortunately, when written, most dialects are understood by anyone speaking Italian.

STANDARD ITALIAN

The official Italian used in business, newspapers, radio and television is the dialect of Tuscany (Florence, to be specific).

The Tuscan dialect became important in the late 13th and early 14th centuries when Florence was at its cultural peak and Tuscan authors such as Dante, Boccaccio and Petrarch began to use it in literary works. Between the Renaissance and the mid-20th century, most Italians still spoke dialect. Only the educated upper classes both wrote and spoke "pure" Italian. Regional dialects proved problematic during World War I when soldiers from different regions had problems communicating. After World War II, the Tuscan dialect became more standardized; it was taught in schools, literacy rates rose and people were exposed to official Italian through now widespread communication systems.

Today, standard Italian is leaning more toward the dialect of Rome. It is said that the finest spoken Italian is *la lingua toscana in bocca romana* ("la LEEN-gwa tos-CAH-nah in BOH-ca ro-MAH-nah") which means "the Tuscan tongue in the Roman mouth," or the vocabulary of Florence spoken with a Roman accent.

ITALIAN WORDS IN OTHER LANGUAGES

The period of the Renaissance and the centuries that followed had an important influence on the cultures of France and England, and many Italian words made their way into the everyday speech of the French and the English. Many of these words are so common today that few people recognize their Italian roots.

While many Italian words have become standard English words, a few English words have found their way into Italian.

Many words that relate to music come from Italian: soprano, libretto, maestro, piano, mandolin and tempo, to name a few. Military terms such as corporal, captain, colonel, artillery and general come from Italian. Some Italian words dating from the 16th century include: zany, sonnet, balcony and cartoon. Other Italian words used in English include: studio, fresco, trio, fiasco, motto, ghetto, solo and incognito—all of which are spelled exactly the same in Italian. And then, of course, there's *ciao* ("chow"), the Italian word for both "hello" and "goodbye," which has been adopted wholeheartedly by many non-Italian cultures.

English words have also found their way into Italian, especially since World War II. Some examples are: supermercato, popcorn, poster, shopping, TV, weekend, party, jeans and cameraman.

SOME ITALIAN SAYINGS AND THEIR ENGLISH EQUIVALENTS

Some of the same ideas behind common English sayings and proverbs have expression in Italian, using different words:

Italian: You're speaking Turkish.
English: It's Greek to me.

Italian: When the cat is out the mice are dancing.
English: When the cat's away the mice will play.

Italian: Better an egg today than a chicken tomorrow.
English: A bird in the hand is worth two in the bush.

Italian: Much smoke but a small roast.
English: Much ado about nothing.

Italian: Drop by drop the sea is filled.
English: Little drops of water make the mighty ocean.

NONVERBAL COMMUNICATION: ITALIAN GESTURES AND THEIR MEANINGS

The Italian language is thought to be extremely expressive and persuasive when spoken. When coupled with the dramatic gestures for which Italians are famous, the language takes on a new dimension.

Probably the most characteristic gesture in Italy (and the one most mimicked by actors playing Italians) is what is known by experts in psychology and nonverbal communication as the "hand purse." This is achieved by holding out the hand with the fingers and thumb touching to create a pocket or "purse." To an Italian, the hand purse indicates a question such as "What are you doing?" "What do you want?" or "What do you mean?" In a tense situation, such as a Roman traffic jam, an irritated Italian might lean out of his car window, hand purse forward, and ask the car in front of him, "What is going on?"

The cheek screw, where the gesturer places his forefinger into his cheek and makes a screwing motion, is another typical Italian gesture. It

The hand purse

The cheek screw

The chin flick

The nose tap

is usually employed to indicate praise or to imply that something is especially good or beautiful. Often, it is used to compliment a good meal—especially a good pasta.

Like almost everything in Italy, gestures have regional differences. To a Neapolitan, an eyelid pull is a warning to be alert. Elsewhere in Italy, it might mean that someone is sly or cunning. In Rome and Naples, to tap the side of your nose is a friendly warning, while in Sardinia it indicates a shared secret. To flick your chin with your hand in the north is a strong dismissive gesture meaning "I couldn't care less;" in the south, however, it is interpreted as a simple, emotionless "no."

A warm greeting for a relative or close friend. However, the handshake is used to greet an acquaintance.

The thumbs up gesture (as in the pilot's "all systems go" signal) was used by ancient Roman emperors seated in the Colosseum to indicate that a gladiator who had fought hard, but lost, should not be killed. Many years later this gesture was reintroduced to Italians as an "okay" sign by American soldiers posted in Europe during World War II. Another American gesture meaning "okay"—the sign made by making a ring with the thumb and forefinger—means "zero" or "the pits" to a northern Italian. To a southern Italian, it is serious insult.

PERSONAL SPACE AND GREETINGS

Italians have few inhibitions about personal space and standing close to one another. They are rarely self-conscious about embracing and it is not unusual to see two men kissing each other on both cheeks or walking arm-in-arm down the street. Women also walk arm-in-arm without thinking about it.

In Italy, the handshake is the standard greeting gesture between acquaintances. The average Italian who runs into someone he knows on the street will stop—even if he or she is in a hurry—converse and shake hands again before progressing to his or her destination. Many younger Italians will stand respectfully when an older family member or friend comes into a room.

TITLES

Signore ("see-NO-reh") and *Signora* ("see-NO-ra") are the Italian equivalents of "Mister" and "Madam" or "Mrs." It is considered impolite in Italy to call an older person or a mere acquaintance by his or her first name until a firmer relationship has been established. It is proper to call an engineer, doctor, lawyer or professor by his or her professional title—*Ingegnere* ("een-jeh-NEH-reh"), *Dottore* ("do-TOH-reh"), *Avvocato* ("a-vo-KA-to"), *Professore* ("pro-feh-SO-reh")—to show deference and respect. *Don* and *Donna* ("Doh-na") are used before the first name of a person who has made an outstanding achievement or for whom one wants to show great respect.

ITALY'S OTHER LANGUAGES

Many Italians are multilingual. People of German heritage living in the South Tyrol speak German as well as Italian. Some 17,000 other inhabitants of the South Tyrol speak Ladin, an ancient language similar to Romansh, one of the national languages of Switzerland.

In Friuli-Venezia Giulia, which borders both Yugoslavia and Austria, various ethnic groups speak German, Croat and Slovene. In Valle D'Aosta, people speak French, while in Calabria and Sicily, many speak Albanian.

ARTS

FOR CENTURIES ITALY HAS GIVEN THE WORLD remarkable examples of artistic accomplishment. The ancient Romans were skilled engineers who built impressive structures throughout the Empire. Italy was the birthplace of the Renaissance and its magnificent architecture, paintings and sculpture. The Italians have given the world the amphitheater and the public bath, the *Mona Lisa* and the *David*, great operas by Verdi and Puccini, the poetry of Dante, the plays of Pirandello, the novels of Ignazio Silone, Alberto Moravia, Italo Calvino and Umberto Eco, the films of Fellini, Bertolucci and others. And Italians today are leaders in the decorative arts; Italian-designed furniture and clothing are highly respected around the world.

The country is said to have more masterpieces per square mile than any other country in the world. Many Italians live with or see great works of art daily without stepping into one of the country's 700 museums. Many of the fruits of ancient and Renaissance architectural splendor still mingle with the modern on Italian streets traversed by people going to and from work. Children play in piazzas crowned by ornate baroque fountains; women worship in churches with art that would proudly be hung on the walls of the world's finest museums.

Opposite: **Venetian masks.**

Below: **Michelangelo's *David*.**

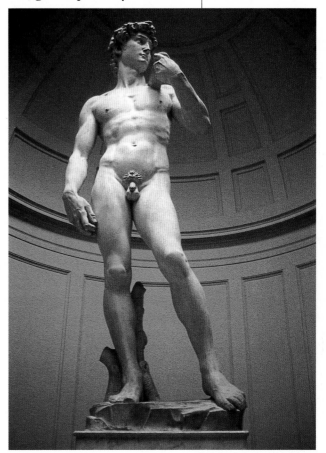

Art in Italy is not confined to museums. Here, in Piazza Navona in Rome, by the fine sculptures of Bernini and Borromini, adults sit meditatively.

For more than 200 years, people have flocked to Italy to see its art treasures: its 30,000 Catholic churches, 20,000 castles and 3,000 historical sites. Writers in particular have come to Italy to escape their own, more conservative cultures, and many have written eloquently about their experience: the novelists Charles Dickens, Henry James, Mark Twain, Herman Melville, E.M. Forster and D.H. Lawrence; the poets John Keats, Percy Shelley, Lord Byron and John Milton. Today, Italy receives some 50 million visitors a year, many of them art lovers who tramp lovingly through Florentine museums, climb the steps of Rome's Colosseum trying to imagine themselves as spectators in ancient times, crane their necks to take in Michelangelo's frescoes on the ceiling of the Vatican's Sistine

Chapel, and stare in awe at Leonardo da Vinci's *Last Supper* in Milan, realizing how magnificent the original is compared to its countless reproductions.

ITALIAN ART: THE RENAISSANCE

Italian artists have contributed much to the world of art over the centuries and they continue to do so, but Italy's finest hour artistically was during the Renaissance ("rebirth") period that took place in the 15th and 16th centuries. The Early Renaissance began in the early 1400s in Florence when artists began to study the ancient Greeks and to adopt their ideas about classical form and proportion. Renaissance artists believed in portraying the human body in an ideal or heroic manner; their figures were very well proportioned and arranged in flattering positions, but they also showed emotion.

Filippo Brunelleschi was the leading architect of the Early Renaissance. Using the classical architectural principles of harmony and balance, he built the first Renaissance building, a hospital in Florence, and some of Florence's finest churches—San Lorenzo, Santo Spirito and Santa Croce. The sculptor Donatello created beautiful, realistic statues of religious heroes, thereby bringing back the long-ignored genre of the free-standing statue. The artist Masaccio was the period's most notable painter. His subject matter often derived from ancient Rome, and his frescoes were remarkable for their use of perspective and their idealization of the human form. Important artists of the late 15th century include: Sandro Botticelli, known for his beautiful, highly-detailed painting, the *Birth of Venus,* in which the modest red-haired goddess of love rises from the sea; and Piero della Francesca, whose frescoes, with their light tones, are filled with graceful figures of exact proportions.

The spirit of the Renaissance achieved its sharpest formulation in art. Art was seen as a branch of knowledge capable of providing humankind with images of God and his creations, and with insights into humankind's position in the universe.

The Renaissance reached its peak in the first part of the 16th century. The High Renaissance, as this era is called, was probably Italy's most creative artistic period, producing such geniuses as Leonardo da Vinci, the architect Bramante, Michelangelo and Raphael. Artists of the High Renaissance were able to work on a grand scale due to the financial support they received from Italy's leading families, like the Medicis of Florence and the Sforzas of Milan, and the popes, who desired to turn the Vatican into a magnificent monument to God and to fill it with important works of art. The colors and textures of the paintings of the High Renaissance are particularly dramatic, due to the use of oil- rather than egg-based paints, a medium introduced by painters from the north.

The *Last Supper* is one of Leonardo da Vinci's finest works. In it, he depicts Christ's last meal and the moment in which he tells his disciples that he knows he will be betrayed. Because Leonardo himself believed in "paint[ing] the face in such a way that it will be easy to understand what is going on in the mind," each of the disciples is given a different facial expression. Leonardo was also an accomplished sculptor and architect, and an engineer by training.

The architect Bramante was commissioned by Pope Julius III to create a plan to rebuild St. Peter's in Rome, today the world's largest church. Much of the actual work on the church was done by Michelangelo, possibly Italy's finest artist. In his frescoes of God and Adam on the Sistine Chapel, his monumental sculptures of Moses and David and his other works, Michelangelo created powerful, heroic, expressive figures whose features are recognized by people around the world. The painter Raphael also embellished the Vatican with his *School of Athens*, a masterpiece depicting the great philosophers of ancient Greece.

Titian's *Venus of Urbino.*

The High Renaissance was represented in Venice by painters Titian, Giorgione, Tintoretto and Veronese, all of whom tended to use a rich palette, and by the architect Palladio, who built classical villas for the wealthy on the outskirts of the city. Many of his elegant homes inspired great English and American architects.

The Late Renaissance period took place in the latter part of the 16th century when the Mannerist style of painting became popular. Mannerism refers to the "mannered" or highly stylized works created during this period by artists such as Pontormo and Parmigianino. Their figures are often highly colored and unnaturally elongated and emotionless—a far cry from the emotional, ideal subjects of Renaissance painters. Mannerism gave way to the Baroque style in the early part of the 17th century, when painters such as Caravaggio and Carracci and the sculptor Bernini adopted a dramatic, asymmetrical style.

ART RESTORATION IN ITALY

On any given day in Italy, the innocent person seeking his or her favorite art treasure may arrive in the piazza, museum or church where it is housed only to find his or her view obscured by iron scaffolding or the object wrapped in a protective green wire mesh. While Italy is home to many of the world's masterpieces, many of them are in a state of disrepair and are currently undergoing important restoration. Leonardo's *Last Supper* was recently renovated because certain sections of the work were flaking off. Piero della Francesca's *Sacred Convention* in Milan is cracking. Many of Rome's ancient monuments are crumbling and the art treasures and churches of Venice, which withstood devastating floods in 1966, 1979 and 1986, are constantly in need of protection from the damp climate. Even the Leaning Tower of Pisa (above), which began to incline just after it was built in the 12th century and continues to incline about eight one-hundredths of an inch a year, may have to be restored.

Restoration is becoming more and more necessary in Italy as works age and as pollution becomes a serious problem in the major cities. Naples alone is said to have 700,000 cars. Dangerous emissions from cars and tour buses (as well as the vibrations the vehicles make) have caused whole sections of marble to fall off important ancient monuments in Rome. The 1986 flood in Venice brought five feet of water into the city's piazzas and into the first floors of museums, churches, stores and people's homes—harming beautiful mosaics and soiling paintings.

A recent study in Italy shows that about 60% of Italians are seriously worried about the decline of their artistic treasures. Unfortunately, the Italian government is unable to finance many restoration projects. The annual budget for the Ministry of Cultural Patrimony in Rome is only $400 million, but it has been accused of spending only half of that—what it costs to build 10 miles of a new highway. Often, corporations and local governments donate money to finance important projects. Computer companies such as IBM and Olivetti have developed computer programs that provide detailed maps of how every

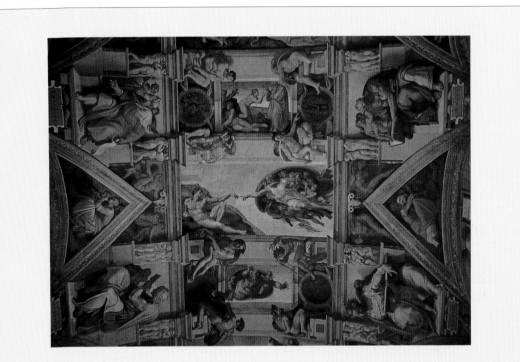

inch of the painting or archeological site originally looked; other companies have donated sophisticated machines that can see below the surface of the paint and scrutinize brushstrokes or sketches that the painter erased.

A Japanese television network, Nippon Television, recently donated $3 million to Italy's most controversial restoration project—the cleaning of Michelangelo's frescoes in the Sistine Chapel (above)—in exchange for the exclusive rights to film the process. The frescoes, it seems, were coated with many layers of soot accumulated over the centuries from the burning of candles. They were also smeared with grease used by former, less sophisticated restorers to impede cracking. As the works have been cleaned, the colors of the paintings have changed. It has now been determined that Michelangelo, known in the art world for his somber shades—deep grays, dark maroons, earthy olives—and subtle shadows, actually painted his famed work in gaudy colors: neon purples, electric greens and yellows, and glowing pinks. Art historians claim that restorers have gone too far in their cleaning efforts, that they have removed the dark shadows that Michelangelo intended as well as years of accumulated grime. According to Giovanni Carandente, an Italian art critic, "Michelangelo must be studied all over again, so revolutionary is this discovery about the painter of whom some had dared to write that in the Sistine he adopted colors that all leaned to brick or gray."

ITALIAN THEATER: THE COMMEDIA DELL'ARTE

During the Renaissance, a new style of theatrical performance developed in Italy called the *commedia dell'arte*, which had its roots in ancient Roman farce. The plays in the *commedia dell'arte* had simple plots: a member of the upper class is tricked by a member of the lower class, for instance, or two unlikely people fall in love. The actors played stock characters who represented certain types of people: Pulcinella, the braggart; Harlequin, the valet; Columbine, the lady's maid; Pierrot, the lover; Scapino, the knave; Scaramouch, the old fox; Pantaloon, the clown; and Mezzetino, the musician. The actors were expected to have many talents; they had to sing, dance, fence and do circus tricks. Audiences laughed uproariously at the antics on the stage as the characters got themselves into and out of all sorts of trouble.

In the 16th century, an Italian *commedia dell'arte* troupe visited Catherine de' Medici in France. This theatrical style later influenced the French farces of the playwright Molière, and became popular in England, Germany and Russia.

ITALIAN MUSIC: THE OPERA

Italy has made a tremendous contribution to the world of music. The Italian language provided the world with its musical vocabulary and the Italians invented the opera. In the late 16th century, a group of Florentine Renaissance musicians and poets began setting poems

The Olympic Theater in Vicenza, built between 1580 and 1582. The theater is still in use today.

to music. The first operas were produced in the early years of the 17th century in Rome, Venice and Naples. As a love for opera swept the country, each city developed its own style. A composer named Monteverdi, considered the father of modern opera, led the Venetian school of composers. Many of his works were presented in Italy's first public opera house, opened in Venice in 1637.

Soon, leading European composers such as Handel began traveling to Italy to study opera. In the late 17th century, Alessandro Scarlatti, who wrote nearly 100 operas, made Naples an operatic center. During the 18th century, the dramatic part of the Italian opera became more important than it had originally been, and the musical segments became more complicated. Europe's most famous opera house, La Scala in Milan, was opened in 1778, and even Mozart began composing operas to be staged there.

The famed summer opera in the Roman amphitheater in Verona attracts many foreign visitors.

The Italian comic opera, or opera buffa, originated in Naples in the 18th century. It developed from the interludes which were performed between acts in serious operas.

The 19th century was Italy's most fertile musical period. Rossini wrote the classic comic opera *The Barber of Seville* in 1816 and Giuseppe Verdi, considered Italy's finest composer, wrote 26 operas including *Rigoletto* (1851), *Il Trovatore* (1853), *La Traviata* (1853) and *Aïda* (1871), the last set in Egypt and performed with such live "props" as camels and elephants. Verdi's operas are praised for the strength of their dramatic plots and well-drawn, realistic characters. Some of his plots were drawn from the works of Shakespeare and Victor Hugo, and his themes often dealt with the struggle of the oppressed. Giacomo Puccini was another significant 19th-century Italian composer. His *La Bohème* (1896) and *Madame Butterfly* (1904) are well-loved today for their romantic, moving stories and melodies.

Italian opera was originally a diversion of the upper classes. With the opening of the public opera house in Venice, it became a source of entertainment for everybody. On opening night, crowds filled the halls and people discussed a new opera for days after they had seen it. In the 19th century, going to the opera was the main social activity for Italians; they came to see and be seen, they often brought food and wine with them to eat and drink between acts, and they even read the newspaper. Those wealthy enough to afford seasonal boxes dropped in every night just to see who else had come or to listen to a particular segment of the opera.

Even today, Italian opera audiences are likely to talk (about the opera or other subjects) during the performance; some people get very involved with the action on stage, and unwittingly offer their comments to others around them. Some even bring picnics to eat during intermission (but not at La Scala). Italian opera stars, such as Luciano Pavarotti, are like soccer heroes who, depending on their performance, can earn either the love or the contempt of their audiences.

FLORENCE: CITY OF CRAFTSMEN

Italy is a country of craftsmen and certain cities and towns have particular areas of expertise: Cremona, in Lombardy, is famous for its master violin makers; Carrara, in Tuscany, has its internationally known marble cutters; Murano, near Venice, is known for its glassworks; and near-by Burano for its lacemakers. Florence, however, is the Italian city most associated with centuries of expert craftsmanship. The city's narrow, winding streets are filled with tiny workshops where the children, grandchildren and great-grandchildren of fine artisans continue to perfect their skills.

Certain workshops are devoted to silversmiths who create intricate figures and pieces of jewelry to order. There are woodcarvers who both carve items for sale and do expert restoration work on the wood in Florence's Renaissance churches. There are metal sculptors, frame-makers and artisans who work in copper, bronze and marble. Many craftsmen in Florence work in leather (some spend nearly a month to craft one beautiful burnished leather box) and gold. The workshops and stores of the goldsmiths have historically been located in the buildings that span Florence's oldest bridge, the Ponte Vecchio (above). There are a few remaining silkweavers in Florence who still work on a type of loom designed by Leonardo da Vinci. To create a length of fabric, the weaver must thread each strand into the loom by hand, even though the pattern consists of 40,000 individual strands! Many of the silkweavers are women whose mothers and grandmothers were also silkweavers in the same workshop.

ITALIAN LITERATURE: DANTE ALIGHIERI

Dante wrote the *Divine Comedy* in exile between 1310 and 1321.

The Italian literary style made its entrance comparatively late in the European world because, before the 13th century, Italian writers composed their works in Latin, the formal language of literary purposes. Dante Alighieri, born in Florence in 1265, was the first poet to achieve great acclaim by writing in the spoken dialect of Florence, Tuscan. Dante's most important work was what he called the *Comedy*, but was later renamed the *Divine Comedy*. It had tremendous influence over Italian literature and is still considered the single finest work written in that language.

The *Comedy* is a poetic work of epic proportions that describes the poet's journey through three places: hell, purgatory and heaven. In each part, the poet seems to adopt a different voice to match the mood of the place he is describing. Along the way, the poet meets the souls of both the sinners and the saved and appears to sympathize with each one, thereby showing the reader the difficulty of choosing the right path. In the *Comedy*, Dante discusses the important issues of his day: politics and its evils, various types of love, the nature of free will, and religious salvation. The poem is an amazing exhibition of the length and breadth of Dante's knowledge as well as an important historical document about the Middle Ages.

ITALIAN ARTS IN MODERN TIMES

Italian artists continued to have a significant impact on the artistic world into the 20th century. Between the 1930s and the 1980s, Nobel prize-winning playwright Luigi Pirandello, and writers Ignazio Silone, Alberto Moravia and Italo Calvino received international attention for their works. Today, the novels of Italian author Umberto Eco, *The Name of the Rose*, a brilliant detective story set in a monastery in the Middle Ages, and *Foucault's Pendulum*, a contemporary story about three editors who

A sidewalk caricaturist. Struggling artists and students of art paint for tourists to make ends meet.

attempt to take over the world, have sold millions of copies in the United States and elsewhere.

In other artistic disciplines, 20th-century Italy produced the painter Amadeo Modigliani, known for his elegant elongated portraits, and the surrealist Giorgio de Chirico, as well as fine composers, opera singers, architects and filmmakers.

LEISURE

ITALIANS TYPICALLY SPEND Sundays involved in leisure activities. Many go to cafés, where they chat with old friends over coffee or wine, discuss politics or argue passionately about the strengths and weaknesses of local soccer heroes. Sometimes just the men go, while the women stay home cooking the Sunday meal. In Italy cafégoers are allowed—even encouraged—to stay as long as they like. They read quietly, write letters, or meet a succession of friends at the same table for hours without feeling pressed to move on.

On Sundays in fair weather, families sometimes gather to enjoy an extended lunch at an outdoor restaurant. They sit for the entire afternoon, praising the good food and wine and, most importantly, conversing about a variety of topics. Young people meet at the local beach or at a designated piazza in the city where they simply hang out and chat.

THE PASSEGGIATA

The *passeggiata* ("pahss-sayd-JAA-tah") or evening stroll is one of Italy's most enduring, civilized leisure activities. Every evening before dinner in many towns, people dress up and stroll through the main square, greeting each other and chatting amicably about the day's events. Sometimes the men sit outside at cafés and admire the passers-by. The *passeggiata* gives everyone a chance to look their best and to see others looking the same. It provides an opportunity to keep in touch with neighborhood goings on and with fellow members of the community.

Opposite and below: **Italians enjoy the simple things in life such as taking a walk, eating a meal and watching the world go by.**

SOCCER MANIA

In Italy—a land of competing regions—a love for soccer (called *calcio* or "KAHL-cho" in Italian) may be the country's strongest unifying factor. A typical Sunday for many Italians is spent at church, a family lunch and, finally, perched in front of the television set to watch a game or two of soccer. According to an Italian soccer fan quoted in *Sports Illustrated* (June 11, 1990), in Italy, soccer "is not just a sport, and it's more than a business. It's a fact of life, like breathing or eating. For Italian men, three things are important—women, food and soccer. But on the day of a big game, the order changes to soccer, food and women. Even Freud couldn't explain this."

Soccer was introduced to Italians in the late 1800s by the British, but it was not until the 1930s, under Mussolini, that the sport took off on an international level. Mussolini felt that a great national soccer team would be a source of national pride, so he saw to it that stadiums were built and teams developed all over the country. Italy has had championship-winning teams ever since.

Today, children in Italy start playing soccer at an early age. Games can be started anywhere, at any time—in a public square, on a small street, in the schoolyard—and anything kickable can be used if no ball is in sight. Italians follow the big soccer leagues with great passion. There are 16 Series A (or First Division) teams within Italy who play each other for the national title. The winner then plays other European national teams. There are four sports newspapers in Italy and headlines are dominated by soccer stories. And about 1,000 hours of soccer games are offered on television each year.

Italians are fiercely loyal to their city's team. Some of the best teams include: Juventus from Turin, owned by Gianni Agnelli, the head of Fiat;

Fiorentina from Florence; and Lazio and Roma from Rome. Some of the finest players are brought in from other countries. Soccer fans get very exhilarated when their team wins and downcast or even personally affronted when they lose. When the Italian national team lost the World Cup in 1986 in fact, a large group of fans met them at the airport—not to help soothe the team's wounds, but to boo and berate them for their failure.

Italian players wear uniforms plastered with the names of their commercial sponsors (candy, pasta, even coffin companies). The fans are known for their ungentlemanly behavior and lack of inhibition when it comes to vocalizing their opinions about the other team or their own players, especially when they are not playing up to par. If a player gets hurt, he is likely to be called a "faker" or an "exaggerator" by the fans, or even an "old man." Sometimes fans display banners with extremely abusive messages on them. They even throw fruit and rocks at the opposing team. When a team wins, its fans are likely to rush on the field and rip the shirts off the winning players.

In the last few years, fans (called *tifosi* or "ti-FO-si," which literally means carriers of typhus, a terrible disease) have become so involved in the game that violence has broken out in the stands and people have been killed. At the 1985 European Cup in Belgium, 39 fans (a majority of them Italian) died in a brawl that erupted in the stadium.

A big turnout for a soccer match. Italian soccer fans are passionately involved with the game and can reach heights of ecstasy or become absolutely despondent depending on whether their team is winning or losing.

BASEBALL AND BASKETBALL

Italians learned soccer from the British and baseball and basketball from the Americans.

Baseball was introduced by the Americans stationed in Italy after World War II. Although the salaries paid to baseball players are not nearly as high as in soccer, and the level of play not equal to that of a professional American team, baseball in Italy is a much-loved sport. Many of the players come from the United States (some from the minor leagues, others as retirees from the majors) and find life as a baseball player in Italy to be very pleasant.

Contemporary baseball in Italy has been likened to American baseball in the 1940s and 50s. The stadiums are smaller and more intimate than most American stadiums. Whole families bring picnic baskets to the ball park and watch the game together. The oldest stadium, in Nettuno, just south of Rome, has very limited seating in concrete stands, with a capacity of only 1,200. (However, some 4,000 people usually squeeze in for the games.) The fans, like those in soccer, are extremely devoted and unhesitatingly vocal, but rarely violent.

Basketball, simply called "bàh-sket," is fast becoming a favorite among Italian children. Some of the most devoted attend expensive basketball camps in the summer; many watch American NBA games on television.

Technically, basketball is still an amateur sport in Italy. Teams play according to amateur rules, thereby qualifying them to compete in the Olympics. However, players do make excellent salaries and are permitted to accept commercial sponsorships. Italian players are often coached by Americans and the best ones are sent to the United States to play on college teams with the promise that they will return to help the team at home.

Summertime at the beach. Most Italians take their vacations in their own country, visiting the places which tourists go to.

OTHER SPORTS, RECREATIONAL ACTIVITIES AND AMUSEMENTS

Italians participate in amateur sports such as horseback riding, running, cycling, swimming, boating and tennis. During summer vacations, families rent small beach or mountain cottages or go to their villas in the country. Skiing is a popular sport in the winter months. There are ski slopes within a few hours' drive from Rome, but the best skiing is found in the Italian Alps. People living in small towns especially enjoy a relaxing type of lawn bowling called *bocce* ("BOH-chay"). Many Italians follow professional cycling and automobile racing with great interest.

Betting has become an obsession in Italy recently. Italians spend some $12 billion a year on gambling—one-third of it illegally. The country has six national lotteries, about 4,700 regional lotteries and thousands of smaller ones. In 1989, Italians bet $2 billion on soccer matches. In one of the most popular games of chance, called Totocalcio, bettors try to guess which soccer teams will win their games on Sunday. Italians also bet on boxing matches and cycling races. Television game shows, where contestants win large amounts of money, are also extremely popular.

The film industry has spawned a new art form, that of the cinema poster. Poster artist Silvano Campeggi is pictured here with one of his works during a retrospective exhibition of his works.

TELEVISION, FILM AND MUSIC

Italians are avid television watchers. Only a few years ago, television was basically a large-city phenomenon; now, people in the remotest villages have sets and much of their leisure time is spent in front of the tube. Italy has a surprisingly large number of channels and a large range of programing to choose from. In the mid-1980s, Rome alone had some 83 privately-owned television stations and Sicily had 123. Italian-produced game shows and news, sports and entertainment programs have traditionally been the favorites but American programing has started to become the rage. Italians love evening soap operas like *Dynasty* and *Dallas* as well as daytime soaps.

The year 1955 was a golden year in Italian filmmaking. Some 819 million tickets were sold and people flocked to the cinemas to see Italian-made westerns (called "spaghetti westerns") and films of epic proportions. Italian directors—Roberto Rossellini and Federico Fellini, to name two—were known the world over. Today, ticket sales have dwindled to about 95 million a year, only about half the movie theaters remain and far fewer movies are being made annually.

Italy still has great directors (consider Bernardo Bertolucci who directed *The Last Emperor*, Giuseppe Tornatore who made *Cinema Paradiso*, and Lina Wertmuller) and Italians still love movies, but now, it seems, they favor Hollywood productions over Italian ones. Teenagers in Italy are the real moviegoers. Their parents and young siblings prefer to watch a movie at home, on television, rather than pay $9 to see one in the theater. Some Italian directors have attempted to remedy this problem by making two versions of their films: one the length of a feature film, the other cut into several episodes to meet a mini-series television format.

Italians are serious opera lovers and feel proud to live in the country where opera began. The opening night (usually the first week in December) at Milan's famous opera house, La Scala, is one of the most exciting social and cultural events of the year. Free concerts of chamber or symphonic music are held in cities and towns of all sizes throughout the year.

THE READING PUBLIC

Although large Italian cities are known for their libraries and bookstores, Italians in general do not read as many books as their northern European neighbors. They do spend a good deal of time reading daily newspapers and illustrated weekly periodicals, however. Most of the nation's 100 newspapers are published in the north. Each of the major cities has one or two newspapers with large circulations; and each of the major political parties publishes a daily paper, as does the Vatican. Newspapers devoted entirely to sports are extremely popular, as are illustrated weeklies featuring articles related to women's topics, the Catholic Church, politics, business and popular culture.

The writing style of many of Italy's most respected papers is said to be notoriously haughty and directed to an intellectual reader. Italian journalists tend to digress and do not hesitate to offer their own, highly idiosyncratic opinions before describing the events that took place. Many Italian newspapers have entire sections dedicated to literary and cultural issues.

FESTIVALS

ITALIAN HOLIDAYS

New Year's Day	January 1
Easter Monday	April
Liberation Day	April 25
Labor Day	May 1
Assumption of the Virgin	August 15
All Saints' Day	November 1
Immaculate Conception	December 8
Christmas	December 25
St. Stephen's Day	December 26

Italians, with their love for elegant costumes, fanfare, ritual and ceremony, are devoted festival-goers and participants. The number of annual festivals in Italy is staggering; some type of festival is usually taking place somewhere in Italy every day. (In the 1970s, in fact, the Italian government decided there were too many festivals, so they abolished seven of them, including the saint's day for St. Valentine.)

Italian festivals can be grouped into many different categories. Many are religious and serve to show devotion to a particular patron saint of a town or village. The participants often wear traditional costumes, play instruments, and display an oversized image of a saint. Other Italian festivals have historical rather than religious origins. They honor certain events—such as the end of a terrible plague—and can be celebrated on a national, regional or local level. These usually include a re-enactment of the event, which often dates back to the Middle Ages or the Renaissance, a costumed procession, and sometimes a mock battle or contest such as a horse race, ball game or rowing match.

[In Italy,] there are [country festivals] that celebrate asparagus, cherries, lemons, strawberries, apricots...; festivals in honor of geese, frogs, ducks and thrushes.... Festivals reenact the primal rhythms of the birth and death of seasons and crops,...the great release of warmth from the sun and of moisture from water that causes crops to be born....Festivals are a key to the secrets of the world."

—*from* Celebrating Italy *by Carol Field*

Opposite: **A religious festival.**

105

The Calendimaggio, a colorful festival celebrated in Assisi, in the month of May.

Some festivals focus on the performing arts: opera, theater, film, poetry or dance. Guest performers are invited to many artistic festivals, even those organized in small towns, to bring culture and entertainment to the locals. Palermo, Sicily, hosts a famous puppet festival each year in November. The best known arts festival in Italy takes place in Spoleto in late June and early July. For three weeks, various international artists perform for thousands of people in locations throughout this ancient town in Umbria. The last concert is held out of doors in front of an 800-year-old cathedral while the audience listens from the church steps.

Other festivals in Italy are organized to celebrate the harvesting of a particular local food or delicacy: the ripening of grapes, the eating of truffles, the making of olive oil, the harvesting of artichokes. Festivals often have special foods or dishes associated with them: roast pork is served on St. John's Day; lamb for Easter in Rome; eel on Christmas Eve; lasagne for Carnival.

Festivals in Italy unite people in a common purpose, reacquaint them with the past, and give them a sense of identity with their communities. Families get together to create costumes, to cook special meals and to watch and rejoice in the festivities. Members of all social classes work together to ready a town for a feast day. Colored lanterns are hung in the main square, tiny white lights strung up to outline monuments or churches, elaborate fireworks displays readied, miles of tables set up in the center of town to accommodate throngs of people who wish to feast together.

Employees are given time off from work to help and soldiers are given leave from the army to attend. In a medieval Umbrian town called Spello, nearly all its 8,000 residents gather to prepare the town each year for Corpus Christi, in June. Together, they "paint" the main street with flower petals, creating enormous, subtly colored replicas of great works of art like Raphael's *Holy Family* or Michelangelo's *Moses*.

Some festivals in Italy are so elaborate that organizers begin preparing for next year's activities just after this year's are completed. Italians celebrate their festivals with great joy and exuberance. Whatever the weather, they gather in the main square in large groups, and dance, sing and feast until dawn.

The living chess game in Marostica. It is watched by thousands of people who follow the moves with great enthusiasm or disapproval. Each move is announced in an ancient Italian dialect.

MAROSTICA'S LIVING CHESS GAME

A real human chess game took place in Marostica, a medieval town in the Veneto region of Italy, in 1454. Two noblemen were ordered by the town's governor to play chess to win the hand of a beautiful girl instead of fighting for her in a bloody duel.

Today, to commemorate the event, each September in even-numbered years, the town's main piazza becomes a life-sized chess board and 500 townspeople dress in rich medieval costumes to represent the pieces in a chess game. Knights wear real armor and ride real horses; castles are small buildings on wheels. Underneath the costumes are ordinary citizens of the town—shopkeepers, students, pharmacists—who practice their parts for six months prior to the performance and who have participated in the game for years, starting as a lowly pawn and moving up to an important king or queen.

Costumed girls at the Venice Carnival.

CARNIVAL

Carnival, which means "goodbye to the flesh," has been celebrated with abandon in Italy for many centuries. Carnival takes place during the 10 days prior to Ash Wednesday, the beginning of Lent, a time of prayer and self-examination when indulgences (such as meat eating and excessive revelry) must be given up.

In the Middle Ages, Carnival-goers would dress in masks, attend costume balls, drink wine and eat rich food to excess. At one time, the Carnival in Venice lasted six months! Masks would assure anonymity for the party-goers and exempt them from any sins they might commit. Today, Carnival is still celebrated with intensity in a few Italian cities, especially Venice and Ivrea.

In Venice, the Carnival ritual was resurrected in the late 1970s. For 10 days, thousands of people gather in the most famous square in Venice—Piazza San Marco—in fair, freezing, rainy or snowy weather, to listen to music, dance wildly, and dress up in elaborate masks and fancy costumes as nuns, popes, witches, knights, soldiers. Entire families roam the streets in search of revelry. Moms, dads and babies dress up in anything from historically accurate Renaissance attire to Cinderella and Rambo costumes. Puppet shows are held, great balls hosted, operas and theater productions performed. People on the streets stage mock battles using shaving cream and anyone participating in Carnival is apt to be coated with the stuff. At the end of the festivities, a huge bonfire is started and an effigy of the King of Carnival is burned, indicating the end of the days of excess and the start of penitence and abstinence.

PALIO IN SIENA

This Tuscan city's most celebrated event, held twice yearly in July and August, has been re-enacted almost without fail since the early 14th century. The festival begins with a slow, dignified procession of people dressed in historically accurate costumes of silk, fur and velvet. Today, the costumes resemble clothes worn in the 15th century, although they change over time. The marchers are representative of the 17 districts that once made up the medieval Sienese Republic. The spectators, who number close to 10,000, wave scarves indicating their fierce allegiance to one of the medieval parishes. Each group makes periodic stops along the route in front of important institutions in the city.

The solemnity of the 90-minute procession is in direct contrast with the wild horse race that follows. Ten jockeys ride bareback around Siena's sumptuous Piazza del Campo. There are no rules in the race and the victor may do anything he needs to win, including striking another jockey. Bribery is even allowed and a horse with no rider can be declared the winner. The winner receives a standard with an image of the Virgin Mary on it and is given an enormous jubilant feast the night after the race. Even the winning horse gets an invitation.

The Palio procession moving through a Siena street decked in colorful flags for the occasion.

FAMILY FEASTS AND FESTIVALS IN ITALY

In Italy, family gatherings are common occasions, probably more so than in the United States, but they take on special meaning during the Christmas and Easter seasons. Outside, the chilly streets of Italy's northern cities come alive in the month of December: shops are decorated in tiny white lights, groups of strolling shepherds playing bagpipe-like instruments make the rounds and roasted chestnuts are available from street vendors. Inside, families set up miniature manger scenes on prominent living-room tables. The figures in the crèche have probably been in the family for generations. Italian crèche figures are traditionally dressed like Italians and the lifelike scenes in which they are placed look more like Italy than Bethlehem, where Jesus was born. Depending on the wealth of the family, the figures can be made of paper, clay or stone.

For children, Christmas is also the excitement of opening their Christmas gifts.

Like Americans, Italians today often celebrate Christmas by setting up a tree in the living room. They also burn a yule log called *ceppo* ("CHAY-po") each night and the children traditionally receive gifts on Christmas Day and on January 6, or Epiphany. The second delivery of presents is said to come from an old, kind fairy called Befana. The good presents, of course, only go to the good children while the naughty ones get nothing but coal and ashes.

Family members living away from home always come back for Christmas. On Christmas Eve, extended families (sometimes numbering up to 70 or 80 people) gather for a multi-course feast that often centers around fish, with eel being the most important dish. (During the Christmas season, fish markets display tanks of live eel to entice shoppers.)

EASTER IN ITALY

Easter festivities in Italy, which usually take place the four days before Easter Sunday, include religious processions that re-enact the life and death of Jesus Christ. The pageants in Sicily are said to be the most remarkable and elaborate.

The Monday after Easter is a national holiday in Italy and is often spent at another family gathering—a picnic, if the weather permits. The day after Easter, the cities empty out and all who are able make a pilgrimage to some grassy spot, spread out a large picnic blanket and cover it with delicious dishes.

Traditional Easter Monday fare includes hard-boiled eggs (which symbolize rebirth), sandwiches, pizza, lamb (a symbol of innocence), salad, sweets, wine and fruit. In Sicily, people eat roasted artichokes, country bread, grilled lamb and a grain dish called couscous. Everybody indulges in Easter sponge cake and tiny molded candies in the shape of lambs. Easter gifts include chocolate eggs and a dough-covered hard-boiled egg in the shape of a doll.

Throughout the meal, the children sing Christmas songs for which they are rewarded with coins or praise from older relatives. After the feast they play an ancient game similar to bingo, and then everyone attends midnight Mass together.

The family regroups the next day, after another Mass, for an enormous Christmas dinner that often begins with an especially rich stuffed pasta dish served in broth, and moves on to a richer Christmas fowl such as stuffed turkey or capon and finally, to traditional regional sweets. Everyone in Italy indulges in a sweet sponge cake at Christmas called *panettone* ("pah-nay-TOH-ne"). The typical *panettone* is made with raisins and dried fruit, but each region has its own version. Some are coated in chocolate, others in toasted nuts.

Although both the Christmas Eve and the Christmas dinner meals in Italy can be called feasts by anyone's standards, in the south, the meal on the 24th is the grandest, while it is the opposite in the north. Many southern families eat holiday dinners consisting of only fish dishes. Some serve nine-course meals while others insist that everyone must eat 13- or 24-course extravaganzas.

FOOD

ITALIANS ARE PASSIONATE about food. They love to eat and consider good cooking an art. They are intensively proud of their cuisine, which originated about 2,000 years ago. Ancient Etruscan tombs were decorated with domestic scenes which included cooking utensils such as rolling pins and pasta cutters. Wealthy citizens of ancient Rome were known to dine in great splendor, as is clear from this account of a feast described in Petronius' *Satyricon*, written in the 1st century:

> "First of all we were offered a pig with a crown of sausages…and homemade bran bread….The next dish was a cold cake with hot honey, over which Spanish wine had been poured….After that we found before us a portion of bear meat….And lastly we were offered soft cheese, fruit mustard, a snail for each person, some tripe, a dish of liver, some smothered eggs, turnips, mustard….Then a bowl of olives in vinegar was passed around….When the *prosciutto* ["pro-SHU-to," cured, thinly sliced ham] arrived, we surrendered…."

The poor, of course, ate much more simply. Their diet consisted mainly of fish, cheese, olives and porridge.

Italians claim to have taught the rest of Europe to cook and they are essentially correct. In the 16th century, Catherine de' Medici brought Florentine cooks to France upon her marriage to King Henry.

Italian food is extremely popular outside Italy. Americans in particular have worshiped spaghetti and pizza for so long that many probably think of these dishes as American. Few people realize that Italy is also responsible for introducing the rest of the world to good ice cream, coffee, French fries and fruit pies—food not often associated with modern Italian cuisine.

"At the table, no one grows old."
—*old Italian proverb*

Opposite: **The fish market.**

A greengrocer's stall. Open fresh food markets are popular in Italy, where women shop daily for the day's supply of food.

GROCERY SHOPPING IN ITALY

Using fresh ingredients is essential to most Italian cooks. Many women shop every day to obtain the freshest available food. There is an open market in each village, and several in large cities. In Rome, every neighborhood has a small market or group of pushcarts filled with fresh, seasonal ingredients. The large markets in Rome are colorful, bustling places. Some stalls sell fresh fragrant fruits and vegetables: varieties of plump red tomatoes, wild strawberries, Italian blood-red oranges. Others offer just-caught fish such as swordfish, tuna, eel, squid and octopus. There are butchers' stalls selling sausages of all sizes, pork, lamb and veal. There are stalls that sell flowers, salad greens, herbs, dried and fresh beans, wild mushrooms, breads, olive oils, cheeses. While marketing, shoppers can stop for a snack at a stall selling prepared foods such as pizza, fried ham and cheese sandwiches or bowls of hot homemade soup. Some of the stalls have belonged to the same family for generations.

A pizza and sandwich shop in the market, where shoppers stop for a quick snack before getting on with their shopping.

Aside from open markets, Italians get their groceries in large, American-style supermarkets complete with convenience food such as dried pasta, sliced bread and canned and frozen foods. Others shop at small specialty stores licensed by the government to sell only a few items. *Panetteria* ("pa-neh-teh-REE-a") sell bread, rolls and other freshly baked goods. *Salumeria* ("sah-loo-me-REE-a") are butcher shops that sell delicatessen items like sausages and cheeses. Dairy products can be purchased at the *latteria* ("lat-te-REE-a"); beef, veal and poultry at the *macelleria* ("ma-cheh-leh-REE-a"); fish at the *pescheria* ("pes-keh-REE-a"); fresh fruits and vegetables at the *fruttivendolo* ("frut-ti-VEN-do-loh"); and canned goods at the Italian version of the convenience store, the *alimentari* ("a-lee-men-TAH-ri"). Marketing in the small specialty shops takes time, but many Italian housewives enjoy doing it every day. They get fresher, tastier food and a quick chat with the shop owners. Busy urbanites often buy prepared food such as roast chicken at a *rosticcerie* ("ro-sti-CHAIR-ee") or "cook-house."

MEALS AND MEALTIMES

Italians eat three meals a day: a simple breakfast, at about 8 a.m., a prolonged lunch, from 1 or 2 until 4 p.m., and a late supper, at about 8 or 9 p.m. Breakfast usually consists of coffee and bread or a roll. Many city dwellers grab a quick breakfast on the way to work. They stop at a café and eat and chat while standing, with a small cup of strong coffee and a sweet crescent roll.

Lunch is the most important meal of the day. If possible, children come home from school, fathers (and mothers) come home from work, and the entire family eats a leisurely, filling, multi-course meal together.

In Italy, as a rule, each course is served separately and the plates are cleared before the next course appears. In some homes, an appetizer or *antipasto* (literally, "pre-food") dish comes out first. This often consists of a cold seafood salad, thin slices of an Italian salami or ham served with melon, or artichoke hearts or mushrooms served with oil and vinegar. The next course is a pasta or rice dish, followed by a main course of poultry, meat or fish, a vegetable and/or salad, cheese, fruit, a light, sweet dessert and coffee. Bread and wine are served throughout the meal.

The evening meal is often similar to the luncheon meal, and can be even more elaborate if visitors are present.

THE ITALIAN TABLE

The typical Italian place setting is made up of three plates resting on top of each other: the top is for the *antipasto*, the middle for the pasta and the bottom for the main course. The Italians do not use butter plates; they simply rest their bread right on the table next to the plate. Napkins are usually made of cloth and used for several days. After the meal, each person folds his or her napkin the long way and puts it back into his or her designated napkin ring.

The flatware on the table consists of a small salad fork and a regular fork to the left of the plate, a knife and a large soup spoon to the right, and a smaller knife, fork and spoon ensemble lying horizontally above the plate—for fruit, coffee or Italian ice cream. Contrary to popular belief, Italians do not use the large soup spoon to act as a miniature support for the fork while eating spaghetti. The skilled Italian eater uses only a fork, which he or she places amidst the heap of noodles and twists—just so—making sure that no strands dangle away from the group. Italians cut fruit with their knife and fork—only cherries and grapes are eaten with the fingers. They even use the knife, rather than their hands, to pick up a piece of cheese and place it on a piece of bread. The knife is also used to push food directly onto the fork.

Lunchtime at the fair. Italians have wine at both lunch and dinner.

The wine glass is found above the plates to the right and, in most Italian homes, will be refilled as soon as it is emptied. Many Italians prefer to drink local wines; others favor internationally known Chianti— red wine grown in the Chianti region, which stretches from Florence south past Siena. Italians drink wine at both lunch and dinner, but they rarely get intoxicated during the meal. They are also not likely to smoke between courses as they feel this hinders their enjoyment of the food.

ITALIAN SPECIALTIES

Italian cooking is wonderfully diverse and creative. Italian food—like the Italian language, the Italian character and Italian politics—can best be described in terms of regions. In the past, northern Italians ate primarily corn and rice, while southern Italians ate pasta. Now, these staples have less strict geographic boundaries. For the most part, the pasta served in the north is flat while that served in the south is tubular, like macaroni. Northern Italian cooks tend to cook with butter, southerners with olive oil. Italian cooks prefer to use ingredients grown right in their own regions and to drink local wines. And each region is famous for its specialties, cooked according to tradition. The finest olive oil comes from Tuscany; the best egg pasta, Italian cheese (Parmesan, of course) and ham (called *prosciutto*) come from Emilia-

An old shop in Bologna selling the sausages for which the city is known.

Romagna; the freshest fish dishes and flakiest pastries from Sicily; and the most delicious rice dishes from the Veneto. Each major city is also known for its culinary delights: the tastiest pizza comes from Naples, the choicest roast lamb dishes from Rome, the richest *minestrone* ("mi-nes-TROH-ne") soup from Milan, the most authentic *gnocchi* ("NYOK-ki," dumplings made from potato flour) and *pesto* ("PES-toh," basil and garlic sauce) from Genoa. Lasagne and *mortadella* ("mor-tah-DEL-lah," sausage flecked with bits of pistachio nuts) are said to be the best in Bologna, while while Florence is supposed to have the best beef dishes.

In Italy, people tend to be conservative in their food tastes; they prefer to eat what they are used to, prepared in a familiar way, rather than to try new things. In fact, there was a general uproar when the first McDonald's opened in Rome in 1986, in the historic Piazza di Spagna. Italian food purists protested outside the restaurant and gave away free spaghetti to remind people of their culinary heritage. Today, that McDonald's is said to be one of the world's busiest, serving more than 10,000 people a day, many of them teenagers. But some Italians have never forgiven its intrusion into Rome's historic district. A group calling itself Slow Food (its symbol is the snail) exists to try to persuade Italians that meals should be leisurely, satisfying, tasty experiences.

RISOTTO IN THE NORTH In the northern provinces of Lombardy, Piedmont and the Veneto, people eat a rice dish called *risotto* ("ri-ZOT-toh") rather than pasta at lunch and dinner. To make basic traditional *risotto*, the cook begins with rice from the Po Valley boiled in a small amount of home cooked broth. As the rice absorbs the liquid, another ladleful is added and the mixture stirred. This procedure is repeated for about 20 minutes until the rice is sufficiently plump. Then the cook adds butter, freshly grated Parmesan cheese and a spice called saffron.

Sometimes, other ingredients like chicken, shrimp, sausage, ham, liver, herbs, vegetables, beans and mushrooms are added. The "national dish" of Venice is *risotto* made with peas. Very special *risotto* dishes are made with white truffles or squid (black ink and all). Just as perfect pasta is served *al dente* or "at the teeth," perfect *risotto* must be served *all'onda*, which means "rippling" or "in waves." According to an old Italian saying, a woman who has hands marked by years of *risotto* stirring will be more likely to find a husband.

Italian cooking is not without outside influences. The cooking in Sicily is said to be Greek in origin, and that of Sardinia Phoenician. The northeastern cuisines show Austrian, Hungarian and Yugoslavian influences. And the Italian pasta is claimed by some to have originated in China.

PASTA IN THE SOUTH Pasta (which means "paste") is part of the daily diet of every southern Italian and many northerners as well. Although the Arabs brought dried pasta to Italy in the 13th century, the fresh varieties had been made centuries before. Pasta was commonly eaten with honey and sugar—tomato sauce was not added until the 17th and 18th centuries. The old-fashioned way of eating pasta was with the fingers, arm held high, head tilted back. Traditionally, pasta was made by hand by the mother of the household, who passed her precious techniques down to her daughters.

Pasta galore. Pasta has been part of the Italian's daily diet since the 15th century.

Amazingly enough, there are more than 500 different varieties of pasta eaten in Italy today, all made with the simple ingredients of flour, water and, sometimes, eggs. Traditionally, the poorer southern Italians made pasta with just flour and water; only the northerners were able to afford the eggs.

The names and shapes of some of the varieties reflect the Italian sense of humor, creativity and playfulness: *spaghetti* means "little strings;" *capelli d'angelo*, the thinnest variety of *spaghetti*, is "angels' hair;" the flatter, wider noodles, *linguine*, translate as "little tongues;" ridged, tubular noodles are called *sedani* or "celery stalks;" and other noodles are called "greedy priests," "little mustaches," "radiators" and "car-door handles."

The various lengths, thicknesses and shapes of the pasta relate directly to how they are cooked and how much sauce they can absorb. The long, thin noodles are best for light sauces, the thicker varieties for heavier meat, cream or tomato sauces. The little shapes such as shells, rings and elbow macaroni are perfect for soups; the larger shells and macaronis, such as *rigatoni,* are stuffed with cheese and baked.

The best pizza is said to come from Naples.

PIZZA FROM NAPLES Pizza is indulged in all over Italy, but its true home is Naples, where pizza chefs apprentice for two to three years before earning their qualifications. Classic Neapolitan pizzas include *pizza marinara,* a cheeseless variety made of oregano, tomato sauce and large hunks of garlic, and *pizza Margherita,* made with tomato sauce, local cheeses and basil. (The latter is named for Queen Margherita of the House of Savoy, who praised it while visiting Naples in 1889.) Both pizzas are drizzled with olive oil before being rapidly baked (for only two minutes!) in a large wood-burning oven shaped like an igloo.

Other less traditional Neapolitan pizzas include the *quattro stagioni* ("KWA-tro sta-JEEOH-nee"), made with mozzarella cheese and four separate sections of mushrooms, seafood, anchovies and capers, and *pizza alla pescatora,* made with a combination of sea creatures such as clams, squid and shrimp. Neapolitans in a hurry buy fried pizza snacks from street vendors who cook them in a kettle of hot oil.

GELATO: ITALIAN FROZEN DESSERTS *Gelato* ("jeh-LA-to") means "frozen" in Italian and is applied to a number of dessert concoctions including sherbet and ice cream. Large Italian cities are filled with *gelateria* that serve such standard ice cream flavors as: *stracciatella* ("strah-chee-ah-TEL-ah," chocolate chip), *malaga* (rum and raisin), *crema* (a kind of vanilla custard), *nocciola* ("no-chee-OH-la," hazelnut), *cioccolato* ("cho-ko-LA-to," chocolate) and *caffè* (ka-FEH). Sherbet is made with peaches, strawberries, raspberries, melon, apples, kiwi and bananas. Some shops even serve such unusual flavors as champagne or avocado sherbet, or *gelato* made with grains, such as rice, or carrots and celery. Italians are said to be much more experimental when it comes to eating exotic *gelato* than in trying a new pasta sauce, for example. They do not hesitate to mix unlikely flavors—sometimes five different ones at a time—in the same dish, and they are often eager to try the newest flavors or combinations at their favorite *gelateria*.

Time out for these cooks, for a little *gelato*.

Italian ice cream is said to be much lighter and tastier than American ice cream. Good *gelateria* use only fresh ingredients, such as fresh fruit or freshly brewed *espresso* ("es-PRES-so") for their coffee ice cream, as well as cream, sugar and egg yolks. Large tubs of fresh ice cream are often displayed with pieces of fruit on top and signs reading "*Produzione Propia*" or "homemade." It is acceptable to taste lots of different flavors before deciding which one (or ones) to stack on your cone.

ESPRESSO: STRONG COFFEE Italians are very choosy when it comes to coffee. The uninitiated might need a coffee dictionary to understand all the different types that can be served in one ceramic cup. Consider:

- *Espresso senza schiuma* ("es-PRES-so SEHN-za shee-oo-mah") is a small cup of very strong coffee served without froth or foam on top.
- *Espresso con molta schiuma* is a strong coffee with a lot of foam on top.
- *Espresso corretto* has a bit of alcohol added.
- *Espresso lungo* ("long") is a slightly larger cup of coffee that takes longer to drink.
- *Espresso al volo* ("in flight") is regular *espresso* served up quickly because the coffee drinker is in a hurry.
- *Espresso macchiato* ("es-PRES-so ma-CHEEA-to," "spotted") is with a drop of milk.
- *Espresso al vetro* ("es-PRES-so al VEH-tro") is served in a glass rather than a cup. (Some Italians think it tastes better that way.)

Cappuccino ("kap-pu-CHEE-no") is *espresso* with hot, foamy milk. It can be served on ice, warm or very hot, "clear," which means with a good amount of milk, or "dark," with just a little milk. Then there is *caffè latte* ("ka-FEH LA-teh"), or coffee with a very high proportion of milk.

Italian coffee is often drunk very quickly, while standing up. In Italy, if you elect not to sit down with your cup, you pay about half the price of a cup of coffee taken to a café table and lingered over. Many Italians simply stand around the coffee bar, chatting with the other customers while balancing their *espresso* cup in one hand and a sweet roll in the other.

The first Westerners to import coffee were the Venetians, in 1615.

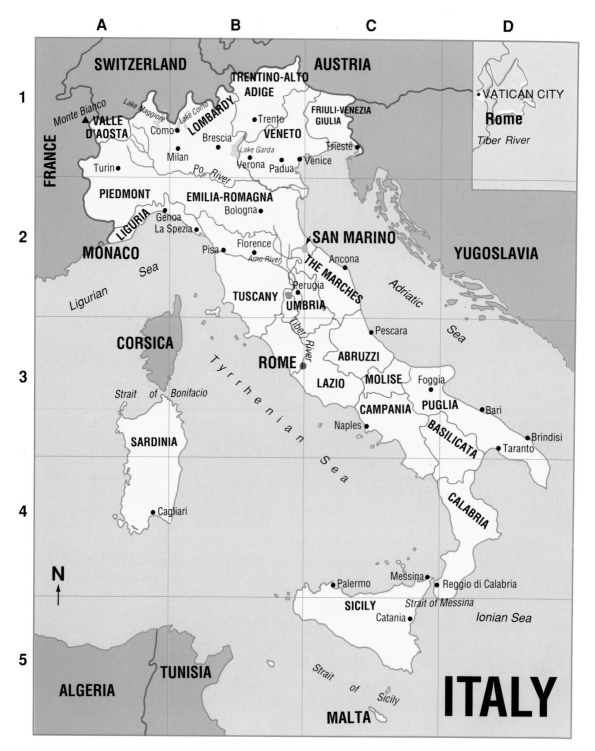

ITALY

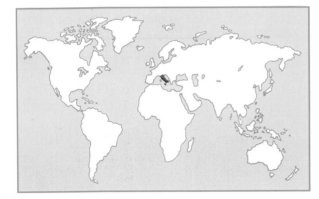

International Boundary
State B0undary
▲ Mountain
● Capital
● City
⟩⟨ River
Lake

QUICK NOTES

OFFICIAL NAME
The Italian Republic (La Repubblica Italiana)

AREA
116,500 square miles

POPULATION
57.5 million

CAPITAL
Rome

REGIONS
Ordinary regions: Abruzzi, Puglia, Basilicata, Calabria, Campania, Emilia-Romagna, Lazio, Liguria, Lombardy, The Marches, Molise, Piedmont, Tuscany, Umbria, Veneto; special regions: Friuli-Venezia Giulia, Sicily, Sardinia, Valle d'Aosta and Trentino-Alto Adige.

IMPORTANT CITIES
Rome, Florence, Venice, Milan, Naples, Turin, Genoa, Bologna, Palermo

MAJOR RIVERS
Po, Arno, Tiber

MAJOR LAKES
Maggiore, Garda, Como

HIGHEST POINT
Monte Bianco (16,000 feet)

MAJOR RELIGION
Roman Catholicism

OFFICIAL LANGUAGE
Italian (Italiano)

CURRENCY
Lira (U.S. $1 = 1,300 lira in August 1991)

MAIN EXPORTS
Machinery, transport equipment, textiles, food products, chemicals, shoes

IMPORTANT POLITICAL FIGURES
Ancient times: Julius Caesar (100 or 102–44 B.C.), dictator of Roman Republic. Augustus Caesar (63–14 B.C.), first Roman Emperor. Constantine (274–337), Rome's first Christian emperor. Charlemagne (747–814), first emperor of the Holy Roman Empire.
Modern times: Giuseppe Garibaldi (1807–1882), Italian independence leader. Camillo di Cavour (1810–1861), forger of Italian unity. Victor Emmanuel II (1820–1878), first king of Italy under unification. Benito Mussolini (1883–1945), Italian Fascist premier. Giulio Andreotti (1919–), present prime minister of Italy. Bettino Craxi (1934–), first Socialist prime minister of Italy.

IMPORTANT ARTISTS, SCIENTISTS AND EXPLORERS
Virgil (70–19 B.C.), Roman poet. Marco Polo (1254–1324), Venetian explorer. Dante (1265–1321), Florentine poet. Masaccio (1401–1428), Renaissance painter. Christopher Columbus (1451–1506), explorer. Leonardo da Vinci (1452–1519), painter, sculptor, architect and engineer. Michelangelo (1475–1564), Renaissance sculptor and painter. Raphael (1483–1520), Renaissance painter. Galileo (1564–1642), astronomer and physicist. Giuseppe Verdi (1813–1901), composer.

GLOSSARY

bella figura   Literally, "beautiful figure or picture;" refers to the idea of making a good impression or showing one's best face to the world.

calcio   Soccer.

al dente   Literally, "at the teeth;" refers to how Italian pasta should be cooked.

gelato   Italian ice cream.

pasta   Literally, "paste;" refers to Italian noodles.

piazza   Town square.

Renaissance   "Rebirth;" period of great artistic, scientific and literary achievement in Italy.

Risorgimento   "Resurgence;" the 19th-century Italian unification movement.

BIBLIOGRAPHY

Barzini, Luigi: *The Italians*, Antheneum, New York, 1964.

Birnbaum, Stephen and Alexandra M. Birnbaum: *Birnbaum's Italy 1991*, Houghton Mifflin Company, Boston, 1990.

Bryant, Andrew: *The Italians: How They Live and Work*, Praeger Publishers, New York, 1976.

Corbishley, Mike: *The Roman World*, Warwick Press, New York, 1986.

Drighi, Laura: *Children of the World: Italy*, Gareth Stevens, Milwaukee, 1988.

Field, Carol: *Celebrating Italy*, William Morrow and Company, New York, 1990.

Grossman, Ronald, *The Italians in America*, Lerner, 1990.

Italy, A Country Study, Area Handbook Series, Foreign Area Studies, American University, U.S. Government Printing Office, Washington, D.C., 1985.

Library of Nations: Italy, Time-Life Books, New York, 1986.

INDEX